A–Z of Play in Early Childhood

A–Z of Play in Early Childhood

Janet Moyles

 Open University Press

Open University Press
McGraw-Hill Education
McGraw-Hill House
Shoppenhangers Road
Maidenhead
Berkshire
England
SL6 2QL

email: enquiries@openup.co.uk
world wide web: www.openup.co.uk

and Two Penn Plaza, New York, NY 10121-2289, USA

First published 2012

A catalogue record of this book is available from the British Library

ISBN-13: 9780335246380 (pb)
ISBN-10: 0335246389 (pb)
e-ISBN: 9780335246397

Library of Congress Cataloging-in-Publication Data
CIP data has been applied for

Typeset by Aptara Inc., India
Printed in the UK by Bell & Bain Ltd, Glasgow

Fictitious names of companies, products, people, characters and/or data that may be used herein (in case studies or in examples) are not intended to represent any real individual, company, product or event.

MIX
Paper from
responsible sources
FSC
www.fsc.org   FSC® C007785

The McGraw·Hill Companies

Praise for this book

"*Janet Moyles consistently provides informed and valuable insights in her writing about the contested world of play. Her work is guaranteed to be informed by watching and listening to children, by her understanding of what they say and think, as well as by her wide-ranging knowledge of significant research in the field. In this, A-Z of Play in Early Childhood, Janet demonstrates her encyclopaedic knowledge of the field which will be of enormous value to those studying play who are looking for explanations, references and cross references. Indeed, the introduction should be used as a base text for those beginning their studies of play. Janet writes in a brilliantly authoritative style as she draws in research and researchers who surround quite contentious and complex issues. This is a scholarly text and is to be trusted.*"

—Dr Kathy Goouch, Reader in Education,
Canterbury Christ Church University, UK

"*In this fascinating and engaging text, Janet Moyles does not attempt to define play. Rather, through a deceptively simple glossary, she illustrates and explores the complexity of play in early childhood. Each entry draws on theory and research from the UK and beyond in order to outline and summarise current thinking and to support further exploration of key ideas. This text will be invaluable to early childhood students and practitioners and to all those interested in extending their thinking about play.*"

—Professor Trisha Maynard, Director, Research Centre for Children,
Families and Communities, Canterbury Christ Church University, UK

"*Those of us who have prepared indexes know about the serendipity of insights gained and new connections made. Here Janet Moyles shares with us her understanding and reflection on play gleaned from many years of writing about (and indexing) play. This book certainly works a useful dictionary to remind us of what (for example) 'epistemic play' means, but I would advise readers to approach it more playfully. The innovative index-as-chapter-heading tempts you to flick across to other sections and Moyles's explanations and*

discursive comments lead your thinking out from the particular en-
try into wider consideration of the importance of play. The imagi-
native use of photographs to illustrate entries, combined with illus-
trative examples, helps to make distinctions between the different
types/aspects of play, and unobtrusive referencing is available for
those who have been inspired to pursue particular interests further."

—Dr Jan Georgeson, Research Fellow in Early Education Development,
Plymouth University, UK

Contents

Acknowledgements

Acknowledgement is due to the following for supplying the photographs:

Photographs C2, D1, G2, K1, L1, N1, S1, V1: Sylvie Gambell, children, staff and parents of the Mary Paterson Nursery School, London
Photographs A1, M3, P1, R3, T1, U1: Ben Hasan, children staff and parents of the Rachel Keeling Nursery School, London

I am most grateful to both these nursery schools for their help and support without which the book would not look nearly as attractive.

Photographs E2 and M2 were supplied by Jenny Cable from Australia who so generously agreed to their use in this book.

And my sincere thanks to Brian who worked his way through each section, commenting and editing as relevant.

Diagrams

Photographs

Tables

Introduction

You can discover more about a person in an hour of play, than in a year of conversation.
(Plato (philosopher) 428–347 BC)

Play is the highest expression of human development in childhood, for it alone is the free expression of what is in a child's soul.
(Friedrich Froebel (founder of the concept of kindergarten) 1782–1852)

The true object of all human life is play.
(G.K. Chesterton (writer) 1874–1936)

The very existence of youth is due in part to the necessity for play; the animal does not play because he is young, he has a period of youth because he must play.
(Karl Groos (evolutionary biologist) 1861–1946)

We don't stop playing because we grow old, we grow old because we stop playing.
(George Bernard Shaw (playwright) 1856–1950)

The creation of something new is not accomplished by the intellect but by the play instinct.
(Carl Jung (psychoanalyst) 1875–1961)

Play permits the child to resolve in symbolic form unsolved problems of the past and to cope directly or symbolically with present concerns.
(Bruno Bettelheim (child psychologist) 1903–1990)

Throughout history, children's play has been observed, discussed, analysed, praised, evaluated and researched but still it seems we do not seem any nearer to comprehending it or valuing it. Can all these eminent people be so wrong about play's significance to children? Is play some reprehensible at-risk behaviour that threatens to make us all lazy? Perhaps part of the problem is that play has always eluded a clear, unequivocal definition – if we could label it neatly then we might be nearer to understanding it. But, as Margaret Lowenfeld said: 'Play in children is the expression of the child's relation to the whole of life; no theory of play is possible that is not also a theory that will cover the whole of a child's relation to life.'[1] 'Play is a multidimensional construct that varies in meaning across time, culture, and contexts.'[2] From pretend play to hopscotch, many diverse behaviours are considered playful, making it notoriously difficult to articulate an all-encompassing definition of play.[3] While play remains elusive in terms of definition, it is, at the very least, a key component of the child's early life, which is why denying play to children can amount to abuse of their rights.

Renowned curricula like the famous *Te Whāriki* put play at the heart of children's learning and development without actually naming or defining it:

> Cognitive, social, cultural, physical, emotional, and spiritual dimensions of human development are integrally interwoven. The early childhood curriculum takes up a model of learning that weaves together intricate patterns of linked experience and meaning rather than emphasising the acquisition of discrete skills. The child's whole context, the physical surroundings, the emotional context, relationships with others, and the child's immediate needs at any moment will affect and modify how a particular experience contributes to the child's development. This integrated view of learning sees the child as a person who wants to learn, sees the task as a meaningful whole, and sees the whole as greater than the sum of its individual tasks or experiences.[4]

This book is not about defining play but exploring, in a basic glossary, some of the different elements of play in early childhood. The idea for the book arose when compiling an index for a previous book on play and the recognition that so many sub-sections were needed after the word 'play' as descriptive and explanatory terms. As such, it is not a book with conventional chapters but one with brief alphabetic sections that outline key aspects of that construct in relation to play. In each section an attempt is made to use some lesser known references and research from international perspectives and some 'different' references; for example, others with expertise in play.

It has been necessary to be selective and finite in the choice of entries; the listings including only those main aspects of play that might arise for students and practitioners which they may want to know a little more about in a ready format. I have tried to avoid contradictions but, as a definition of play continues to be elusive, elements may appear to challenge each other: this is inevitable. Similarly, a book like this cannot be comprehensive; for example, a whole book and more would be needed to explain the relationship between recent and ongoing neuroscience research and babies' and young children's play: here we have only 500–600 words! The majority of the entries give a brief outline but that is not to undermine the complexities of many play concepts and constructs. For this reason all entries have been supported through the use of others' theories and research from international contexts which it is hoped the reader will follow up as relevant to their needs to supplement the necessarily brief information available here. It has to be acknowledged that there are no 'truths' in any study of play; only the possibility of detailed expositions of what we currently know and think.

The stance taken in this book is that play is vital to children's holistic development, self-efficacy and well-being – for that, I make no apology. This positive view of play is taken because of what I have observed over many years – and continue to observe as often as possible – of children playing, both in preschool settings, early years classrooms, out in the park and in my own and others' homes. The argument that play is not the only way children learn are important – anyone only has to see a child prodigy of four play a violin or piano – but do not, to my mind, take away the essential ingredient which is that all learning and teaching should be at least playful in order for children to develop enthusiastic dispositions to learning and school-based activities (see Diagram Intro 1). While current school readiness concerns are

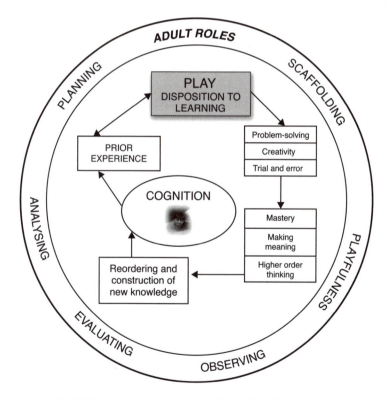

Diagram Intro 1 Children's play and learning and the roles of adults

pushing educators further and further away from playful provision, it is up to early years practitioners to preserve as many opportunities as possible for children to play from their own perspectives.

Gitlin-Weiner proposes that the primary functions of play are 'biological (learning basic skills and experiencing kinaesthetic stimulation), interpersonal (acquiring social behaviours), socio-cultural (exploring cultural roles and rehearsing individual ones) intrapersonal, including mastery of conflicts, negotiation.'[5] When play-based learning is denied in early childhood, this has been reported as presenting later problems from poor job prospects and marriage breakdowns (as reported in the *HighScope* literature[6]) to criminality, as reported by Stuart Brown of the *Institute of Play* in the US, who has studied convicted murderers in Texas prisons and found that the absence of play in childhood is an important predictor of criminality. He is adamant that play is vital to our mental health and well-being throughout our lives: that play is a force that enables us to discover our most essential selves and to find fulfilment and growth.[7]

Doubtless, there will be entries that readers will feel should be included and entries which are included which are felt not to be so necessary: so it will always be with something as complex as play and attempting to condense it into something manageable. The choice of topics will also be a bit idiosyncratic and dependent on the interests and knowledge of the author. The vast number of studies on play show without doubt that words have contextual and cultural meanings and definitions that may be contestable. In some cases, examples have been given to highlight aspects of that particular element of play and photographs are also used in support.

Being swamped as we regularly are in the UK with policy initiatives and current confusions about the value of play and playful pedagogies especially in the 3–6-year age group – and bearing in mind that this equally applies in the US and some other Western societies – the entries have been considered with international perspectives in mind. However, please do not look for definitions of structured/unstructured play: I do not subscribe to structured/ unstructured notions of play so you will not find references (other than here) to this idea. In my opinion, all play is structured by the context and materials; for example, if children have sand available they will run it through their fingers, make piles (wet or dry) and so on. Thus the play in which they are engaged is structured by the materials and the environment. 'Structured' play often means 'guided play;' that is, the adults are guiding the children's play. 'Unstructured' usually means the children doing whatever they want to do with whatever materials but, somehow, has connotations of vagueness or being amorphous that very much understates and underestimates the power of children's play in their making sense of the world and in their holistic development. Play, in adult terms, can be 'guided' but it is as well to remember that, unless and until the children take ownership over that play, it is not really play at all, however playful. Practitioners must learn how to play with children on their terms, assuming a role in pretend play, taking an interest, offering suggestions and engaging eagerly as co-players when invited.[8]

Playfulness is important because it bestows a unique approach to pedagogy that allows all children to engage with the adult in a child-oriented way even if they are not wholly playing. The key ingredient in play is engagement: engagement within your own mind, with another person, or with an object. Play is always a dynamic experience. This type of play is not always possible to achieve in early years settings but being playful can and is vital, for example, for putting a new child at ease or enabling a child with individual or special needs to become involved.

Exhibiting playfulness as a practitioner can also help the few children for whom play does not necessarily come easily, perhaps because of culture, family background or disability. It is also much more fun for the practitioner and makes 'work' much more pleasurable (see Diagram W1, p. 157). Practitioners must value play practices themselves; without a positive play ethic, a playful climate for children's learning and development is spoken of as important, but is not acted upon.[9] One recent study found that overwhelmingly practitioners spoke about the importance of play for children in reception classes but observation of classroom practices revealed little real play taking place.[10]

Example 1

Five 4-year-olds are sitting around a table having been called there by the practitioner. In front of each child is a plastic letter 'b' and a sheet of paper. The adult (upside down to most of the children) demonstrates how to lay the 'b' on the paper and draw around it – this week's sound is 'b.' Each child does as asked: one puts the letter back to front (making 'd'), another lays the letter on its back, another puts it upside down (making 'p') and yet another puts it upside-down and back to front (making 'q'). Each one is asked to turn the sheet over and 'try again properly' at which point the practitioner ensures that all the letters are the right way up and facing the correct way and gives praise. Children then colour in the letter and find three things off 'b' table to be drawn under the letter. The whole activity takes 25 minutes and the children continually fidget and ask with each drawing if they have 'finished now.'

The practitioner felt that this was 'guided play' because the children were fetching things from the 'b' table and placing them down in front of them to draw. But what would this activity actually **mean** to the children? What would they have learned? Would they have perceived it as play? The answer is clearly 'No' to the latter question and, had they been asked, it would have been clear to the adult that the activity had little meaning or relevance to these children and that they only learned that there is a correct way to do something that gets approval.

It would seem that the culture of accountability dominates thinking at the expense of children's play and playfulness and the creative art of the teacher.[11] Penelope Leach suggests that it is 'important that people see early learning as coming from inside children because that's what makes clear its interconnectedness with play ... and play, *real* play, is the other foundation of the early years [author's italics].'[12] Singer and Singer (2005) claim: 'play, in its many forms, represents a natural, age-appropriate method for children to explore and learn about themselves and the world around them.'[13]

So what would the above example have looked like if the adult had used more playful teaching and learning strategies – even real play?

Example 2

Because many of the children are going on holiday to the seaside shortly, the practitioner and a group of five 4-year-olds are, at the children's request, turning part of the outdoor play area into a beach. Earlier the children had brought in from home collections of 'beach toys;' for example, big balls, buckets, spades, shells, small flags, boats and even a bottle of suntan cream! The practitioner adds other things including books. The children play freely with the sand and water but gradually the play begins to form into a story about going away, getting in a car ... the children fetch chairs to make a car and, having assigned roles of mummy, daddy, baby, dog and children, they talk of preparing for the journey and fetch soft toys and 'sweets' from inside the classroom. Meantime, after a short observation, the practitioner fetches baskets and to one attaches the letter 'b.' She tells the children how much she needs a holiday so they invite her and get another seat for the car assigning her the role of 'teacher!' She offers them the baskets for taking all their things and keeps the 'b' basket for herself. She wonders out loud if they should make some lists so that they do not forget anything and Tara fetches some paper and pencils and they all start to write letters on the paper and put them in the baskets. Bevin asks why the practitioner's basket says 'b' on it. The teacher asks if they can put all the 'b' things in her special basket as she would like to carry those: Bashir wants to know if he should go in the basket! After much discussion the appropriate 'b' things are put into the basket. This prompts another game of writing letters for the other baskets especially 's' for sweets! There are groans all round when it is time to tidy up.

Whatever adults participate in will be acknowledged as 'valuable' by children who essentially want to please. In episodes such as Example 2, the adult is acknowledging the children's play and also acknowledging their competence and motivation. Play such as this is authentic learning because it helps children to understand and not just to memorize. As a social act, this play episode ensured children were also learning from each other. Until children are developmentally ready to understand what letters and words represent and that they have meaning, there will be no comprehension – at least, in Example 2, the children could see a point in putting letters on baskets and did so with purpose. Rogers (2010) urges educators to try to view play from the child's perspective.[14] Once they do, the realization of what makes sense to the child on which can be built learning and understanding quickly follows. Much learning in play is implicit – in settings and schools adults need to make it more explicit and make notes of the learning that happens in examples such as Example 2 rather than being intent on worksheet production as in Example 1. As Elkind (2007) stresses: 'Learning is the product of play-generated experiences limited only by the child's level of intellectual development'[15] – it would seem that if we limit children's play, then we limit their development too.

Photo Intro 1 If we limit children's play, we limit their potential

However, it has to be acknowledged that there are only a small number of hours in a day when children are in settings and schools and practitioners are paid to ensure that these hours are productive, educative and, hopefully, fun. 'Play is a child's world and adults who take it over are denying children's need to invent it for themselves. Yet children benefit from adults' ideas and adults benefit from being free to do things they like to do.'[16] An adult's role is 'in setting the stage, adding props and dramatic ideas, helping with problem solving, observing and talking about children's good ideas … It's a delicate balance sustained primarily by observing children, observing oneself, and being open to questions ….'[17] The benefits attributed to play – including learning how to take the psychological knocks of life and learning – outlined in the sections of this book mean that children need time for play as essential to their healthy neurological development and flexibility of mind, more than they need drilling and testing. To keep taking her temperature will not make an ill child better – but playing might!

The twenty-first century has seen many changes in children's lives – in childhood in general. Neurological science has given us new and intriguing insights into the way children learn and, on the whole, this supports play as fundamental in children's lives and education. New technologies mean that the way children play is under threat or being enhanced depending on how we view the likes of the Nintendo Wii, PlayStation and computer games in general. Ways of communication have both expanded and diminished for young children. Television means that children can access the world in ways not possible before its advent but also that children's learning can be very static and limited: first-hand experiential learning is still felt to be the most appropriate form of learning and any virtual learning via television or computer games restricts real-life active learning.

> Our senses are very disordered in the present because the surrounding world has been largely replaced by a simulated world, a world of humanly constructed objects of every type imaginable, *which changes our experience from that of sensing the fullness of the world to being overwhelmed by sensory objects which capture our awareness* [author's italics]. And if our senses do not give us access to the true, authentic qualities of the world, then we merely become surrounded by artificial, materialised representations.[18]

On the other hand, some believe that new technologies fundamentally support children's play and learning particularly in literacies.[19]

It is acknowledged that this book represents only one main view of play that takes place in a particular place, space, time and culture – the culture of early childhood education in 2012/13. The play outlined herein is intended to help the reader understand the 'shifting sands' that are play, to encourage readers to be open-minded, flexible and, yes, playful. There are no assurances in play because of just this flexibility and changeability so each of us has to make up our own minds about the value – or otherwise – of play to ourselves and to the children whom we care for and educate. The choices made in this book reflect the author's own commitment to play and the inclusions are based on that conviction.

References

1. Lowenfeld, M. (1991) *Play in Childhood*. London: Mac Keith Press (first published in 1935, London: Gollancz) (p. 23).
2. Cohen, D. (2006) *The Development of Play* (3rd edn.). Hove and New York: Routledge (p. 18).
3. Tamis-LeMonda, C., Uzgiris, I. and Bornstein, M. (2002) Play in parent-child interactions. In M. Bornstein (ed.) *Handbook of Parenting* (2nd edn.) *Vol. 5: Practical Issues in Parenting*. Hillsdale, NJ: Lawrence Erlbaum (p. 236).
4. New Zealand Ministry of Education (1996) *Te Whāriki: Principles of Learning and Development in Early Childhood*. Wellington: Ministry of Education.
5. Gitlin-Weiner, K. (2006) Clinical perspectives on play. In D. Fromberg and D. Bergen (eds) *Play from Birth to Twelve: Contexts, Perspectives and Meaning* (2nd edn.) New York and London: Routledge (p. 354).
6. Schweinhart, L., Montie, J., Xiang, Z., Barnett, W.S., Belfield, C.R. and Nores, M. (2005) *Lifetime Effects: The HighScope Perry Preschool Study Through Age 40*. Monographs of the HighScope Educational Research Foundation No. 14. Ypsilanti, MI: HighScope Press.
7. Brown, S. (2008) Pilot study of young murderers. Hogg Foundation Annual Lecture. Austin, Texas.
8. Hewes, J. and the Canadian Council on Learning (2006) *Let the Children Play: Nature's Answer to Early Learning*. Montreal, Canada: Early Childhood and Learning Knowledge Centre. Available online at www.ccl-cca.ca/childhood learning (accessed 1 February 2012).
9. Moyles, J. and Adams, S. (2002) *StEPs: Statements of Entitlement to Play*. Maidenhead: Open University Press.
10. Moyles, J. and Worthington, M. (2011) *The Early Years Foundation Stage Through the Daily Experiences of Children*. Occasional Paper No. 1, TACTYC: Association for the Professional Development of Early Years Teachers. Available online at www.tactyc.org.uk.
11. House, R. (2006) Toxic childhood, *The Teacher*, London: National Union of Teachers (p. 14).
12. Leach, P. (2011) The EYFS and the real foundations of children's early years. In R. House (ed.) *Too Much, Too Soon: Early Learning and the Erosion of Childhood*. Stroud: Hawthorne Press (p. 27).
13. Singer, D. and Singer, J. (2005) *Imagination and Play in the Electronic Age*. Cambridge, MA: Harvard University Press (p. 28).

14. Rogers, S. (2010) Play and pedagogy: a conflict of interests? In S. Rogers (ed.) *Rethinking Play and Pedagogy: Contexts, Concepts and Cultures*. London: Routledge.
15. Elkind, D. (2007) *The Power of Play: Learning What Comes Naturally*. Philadelphia, PA: Da Capo Press (p. 103).
16. Jones, E. (1993) *The Play's the Thing: Styles of Playfulness* (pp. 28–30). Child Care Information Exchange. Available online at www.childcareexchange. com (accessed 5 February 2012) (p. 30).
17. Jones, E. (ibid.)
18. Sardello, R. and Sanders, C. (1999) Care of the senses: a neglected dimension of education. In J. Kane (ed.) *Education, Information, and Imagination: Essays on Learning and Thinking*. Englewood Cliffs, NJ: Prentice-Hall/Merrill.
19. Willett, R., Robinson, M. and Marsh, J. (eds) (2009) *Play, Creativity and Digital Cultures*. New York and London: Routledge.

A

Active learning through play

Active learning through play is closely related to experiential learning for young children; the basic need to experience things for oneself through action and all one's senses. The old adage 'I hear and I forget, I see and I remember, I do and I understand'[1] could well have been written for young children – and their educators. Most children are innately active: nature seems to be aware that it is the most preferred mode of 'being' for babies and young children.

Action is not only about physical movement; it is also mental action – the brain must be actively engaged if remembering and understanding are to take place. Recent US research confirms that not only do children learn by doing and that action is the child's preferred mode of learning, but also that physical activity stimulates the brain much more than sitting still.[2] Being active feeds oxygen, water and glucose to the brain, heightening its performance. Active learning also creates more neural networks in the brain and throughout the body, making the entire body a tool for learning.[3]

Play has a huge role for the young in ensuring that they are active both physically and mentally. In the ostensibly simple act of bouncing a ball, a child is both physically and mentally co-ordinating actions and might also be learning that different actions can make the ball bounce higher or move in different directions.

The famous US HighScope programme is based on children's active learning and defines it thus: 'Active learning is . . . learning in which the child, by acting on objects and interacting with people, ideas, and events, constructs new understanding.'[4] HighScope takes this further by incorporating children's thoughtful reflections on their own actions as a means of consolidating both physical and mental learning.

Photograph A1 Active learning means both mind and body are active

Kinaesthetic learning is closely related to active learning: Gardner defines the core elements of kinaesthetic Intelligence as the ability to use one's body in highly differentiated and skilful ways for creative and expressive purposes and the ability to work adeptly with objects, both those that involve fine and gross motor movements.[5]

Example A1

Thomas, aged 1.2, is sitting with a wooden spoon and a saucepan his Gran has given to him. He waves the spoon around and, accidentally, it lands heavily on the pan. He looks about to cry at the loud noise but moves the spoon near the pan again and, this time, gets a gentler sound. Thomas continues to bang getting different sounds dependent on the strength of his action. He hears, sees and feels the effects of his actions and, we can speculate, learns much about cause and effect!

It is acknowledged that boys particularly are more engaged with learning when they are able to play and be physically active. This is due not only to brain development, but also to male sex hormones (androgens).[6] Other researchers provide evidence that boys, who on average have a slower rate of maturation, show significant physical and other differences from girls that affect their responses to early education.[7] Boys seem to need more opportunities for physical play activities than are generally available in reception classes.[8]

Both active and kinaesthetic learning present a strong argument against young children's use of electronic toys and computers that, at best, offer very limited sensory experiences. For example, actively exploring the outdoors presents sights, sounds, textures and smells enabling the learning of scientific principles in a way that no two-dimensional media possibly could.[9]

Adult-initiated/guided play

Adult-iniated/guided play differs considerably from child-initiated play in that the child may or may not perceive the activity to be 'play' at all! There are other terms that could be included here, for example, adult-guided, adult-led, adult-chosen, adult-directed, adult-inspired and adult-managed, all of which differ slightly but essentially mean adult ownership.

Adult-initiated play activities usually have a learning intention in mind and have an end result. The adult may or may not be involved in the play once it has begun but might need to model play for some children. The adult is mainly a facilitator, stimulating, challenging and enriching the children's experiences and providing the resources and context. If the children take ownership of the task, then it may become play. Adult-guided tasks and experiences allow the adult to extend and assess children's learning in ways that may be described as 'playful' rather than play. The challenge for educators is to achieve an appropriate balance. Many people believe that adult-initiated or adult-guided play should occupy only a small amount of children's time, if any (e.g. Bruce[10]), whereas others believe that children will not progress without some adult direction (e.g. Early Years Foundation Stage), which states 'The EYFS requires providers to ensure a balance of child-initiated and adult-led play-based activities. Providers should use their judgement and their knowledge of the children in their care in deciding what the balance should be.'[11]

Example A2

In Little Acorns Nursery the day is structured for the 3–5-year-olds to allow for two periods of adult-initiated play. The observed morning session shows the practitioner initiating the children in how to create sounds from a range of musical instruments. Following 10 minutes of adult-initiated and guided activity, the practitioner leaves the group of four children to play with the musical instruments. At first, they simply make loud noises but, gradually, the children form themselves into a 'band' and snake their way through the nursery corridors pretending to be at a parade (they've seen one the previous week in their local village).

Adult-initiated play is relatively easy to set up – the best practice arises when the children are able to take ownership of the task, thus enabling it to become true child-led play as in the example.[12]

The BERA Report concluded:

> Pedagogy based on play is difficult to achieve in a context of pre-scribed outcomes but young children learn most effectively in set-tings where the curriculum is planned and they are taught inform-ally, learning through a balanced combination of child-directed and adult-initiated activity.[13]

Adult play

Adult play occurs far more often than we might imagine. As I have writ-ten elsewhere,[14] there is the obvious play of adults involving leisure activi-ties such as games and sports, but there is also, for example, the matter of playing with ideas, playing different roles for different audiences and see-ing the funny or ironic side of things (humour). The importance to adults of play and playfulness can be directly reflected in how they react to, and interact in, children's play: the most enthusiastic adult players will almost certainly value children's play more highly than those who see play as sim-ply frivolous and unworthy. 'Playfulness helps us be more inventive, smart, happy, flexible, and resilient. A sure (and fun) way to develop your imagina-tion, creativity, problem-solving abilities, and mental health is to play with your romantic partner, officemates, children, grandchildren, and friends.'[15] Playful adults, including early childhood educators, inspire playful, creative children.

As Stuart Brown suggests: 'What do most Nobel Laureates, innovative en-trepreneurs, and most successfully adapted mammals have in common? They play enthusiastically throughout their lives.'[16] Consider also this assertion:

> Life without play is a grinding, mechanical existence organized around doing the things necessary for survival. Play is the stick that stirs the drink. It is the basis of all art, games, books, sports, movies, fashion, fun, and wonder – in short, the basis of what we think of as civilization. Play is the vital essence of life.[17]

For adults and children, Sutton-Smith notes the differences between play and work and claims: The opposite of play is not work, it is depression.[18]

Sometimes adult play is dangerous; for example, extreme sports, such a sky-diving, activities perceived as having a high level of inherent danger and risk. Extreme sports are about exhilaration and the control (or otherwise!) of skill and danger. As Tricia David suggests:

> ... in adulthood, play has a central role in the forming and sustaining of relationships. Much adult play may be rule-bound, but much is still free – think of young couples in the early stage of a relationship, or drama groups. Nobel scientists have remarked that their discoveries have often happened during playful imaginings with colleagues. Authors, painters, composers and entrepreneurs play with words, materials, notes and ideas and their work comes alive when they share it with others.[19]

Assessment and play

The younger the children the less likely they are to be able to tell you about themselves; for example, their likes, dislikes, relationships or learning styles. Observing, documenting and analysing children's play is a means of assessing accurately different aspects of their development. For young children perceived to have 'problems,' play is used as the context for evaluating and determining any necessary interventions: 'Play as an assessment/intervention context is relatively new in the field of school psychology but is increasingly popular with practitioners and researchers because of the current emphasis on ecologically valid assessments, context based interventions, and progress monitoring.'[20] Many different aspects can be assessed through play, such as communication skills, and physical, social and emotional development as well as cognitive functioning.

Assessment through play is an essential tool in the repertoire of excellent early childhood educators. It mainly takes three forms: summative, formative and ipsative, of which the latter two are most likely to be used in early education. Summative (normative) assessment tends to come at the end of a learning process and is associated with tests and school/setting comparisons. Formative assessment (criterion referenced) is part of the learning process and is ongoing and continuous, assessing the child against previous learning. Ipsative relates to assessment of children's individual holistic development.

In some Western societies – for example, England and the US – assessment is often linked to audit and accountability, with a current emphasis on 'readiness'[21] associated with preparation for school rather than the child's current needs. Many Scandinavian countries and, in particular, the *Reggio Emilia* and *Te Whāriki* approaches (Italy and New Zealand, respectively), use 'methods of assessment that challenge educators in positive ways. They have to look closely at what children are seeing, saying, doing and knowing in order to understand, celebrate and elaborate learning. The assessment then leads to new levels of challenge for children ... worthwhile activities [which] offer and extend opportunities for holistic growth.'[22]

While various psychological tools exist for the purpose of assessing children through play, in early childhood settings assessment often takes the form of observing play (with or without the use of electronic recording, e.g. cameras) and keeping records so as to assess progress and development. The use of children's 'Learning Journey' logs and similar records of their play experiences is now widespread in early years settings. Some early educators also use a 'Learning Journey Profile' to record their playful interactions with children and reflect on the quality and outcomes of their playful pedagogies.[23]

The motivational aspects of play ensure the highest level of each child's functioning. Assessment will usually involve those within the setting/school and parents in order to gain a full picture of the child's play experiences and responses. The purposes of assessment through play are to link observation of children's current levels of development with the planning cycle (see Diagram A1).

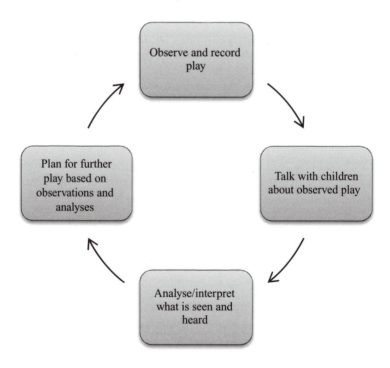

Diagram A1 Assessment and planning cycle

This cycle shows that, when educators understand children's present knowledge and experiences, it is easier to decide what play experiences to provide. As educators assess children's play, they are also reflecting on their own professional skills in knowing what works with individual children and how to provide for higher-quality play experiences.

Autotelic activity

Autotelic activity is any activity including play pursued for intrinsic, self-rewarding reasons. Autotelic play is play for its own sake without extrinsic reason or reward so a person does not play to win but plays for the challenge. Research shows that autotelic play enhances a child's sense of agency and self-worth, which can advance skills in more formal areas as a child develops, particularly creativity and social interactions.[24]

References

1. Confucius (551 BC–479 BC).
2. Jensen, E. (2008) *Brain-based Learning: The New Paradigm of Teaching*. Thousand Oaks, CA: Corwin Press.
3. Hannaford, C. (2005) *Smart Moves: Why Learning is not all in your Head*. Salt Lake City, UT: Great River Books.
4. Hohmann, M. and Weikart, D. (1995) *Educating Young Children*. Ypsilanti, MI: HighScope Press and Educational Research Foundation (p. 17).
5. Gardner, H. (1993) *Multiple Intelligences*. New York: Basic Books.
6. Berk, L.A. (2002) *Infants and Children. Prenatal through Middle Childhood* (2nd edn.). Boston, MA: Allyn & Bacon.
7. Sax, L. (2006) *Why Gender Matters*. New York: Broadway Books.
8. Sanders, D., White, G., Burge, B., Sharp, C., Eames, A., McEune, R. and Grayson, H. (2005) *A Study of the Transition from the Foundation Stage to Key Stage 1*. London: DfES Research Report SSU/2005/FR/013.
9. Elkind, D. (2007) *The Power of Play*. Philadelphia, PA: Da Capo Press.
10. Bruce, T. (1991) *Time to Play*. London: Hodder & Stoughton.
11. EYFS (2008) *Practice Guidance for the Early Years Foundation Stage*. Nottingham: DCSF (p. 7).
12. See also Moyles, J. (ed.) (2010) *Thinking About Play: Developing a Reflective Approach*. Maidenhead: Open University Press (Ch. 1).
13. BERA (2003) *Early Years Research: Pedagogy, Curriculum and Adult Roles, Training and Professionalism*. London: BERA.
14. Moyles, J. (1989) *Just Playing? The Role and Status of Play in Early Education*. Maidenhead: Open University Press.

15. Kemp, G., Smith, M., DeKoven, B. and Segal, J. (2009) *Play, Creativity, and Lifelong Learning*. Available online at http://helpguide.org/life/creative_play_fun_games.htm#authors (accessed 21 December 2011).

16. Brown, S. (2010) *Statement Made Through the Institute of Play*. Available online at http://www.nifplay.org/vision.html (accessed 21 December 2011).

17. Brown, S. with Vaughan, C. (2010) *Play: How It Shapes the Brain, Opens the Imagination, and Invigorates the Soul*. New York: Penguin Group.

18. Sutton-Smith, B. (1997) *The Ambiguity of Play*. Cambridge, MA: Harvard University Press.

19. Tricia David (2011): personal communication.

20. Kelly-Vance, L. and Ryalls, B. (2008) Best practices in play assessment and intervention. In A. Thomas and J. Grimes (eds) *Best Practices in School Psychology* (5th edn.). Bethesda, MD: National Association of School Psychologists.

21. See Whitebread, D. and Bingham, S. (2011) *School Readiness – a Critical Review of Perspectives and Evidence: Occasional Paper 2*. TACTYC: Association for the Professional Development of Early Years Educators.

22. See Luff, P. (2012) Challenging assessment. In T. Papatheodorou and J. Moyles (eds) *Cross-cultural Perspectives on Early Childhood*. London: Sage Publications (Ch. 10, p. 143).

23. Williams, B. (2010) Reflecting on child-initiated play. In J. Moyles (ed.) *Thinking About Play: Developing a Reflective Approach*. Maidenhead: Open University Press (Ch. 5).

24. Petersson, E. (2007) Ludic engagement designs for all, *Digital Creativity*, 19(3): 141–52.

B

Baby play

Play is a main way in which we all learn about our worlds, especially babies and toddlers. It might seem that babies can do little but we now know from brain research just how much is going on from the moment they enter the world (and before).[1] It is during the first three years that trillions of new synaptic connections are made in the brain, influenced greatly by the environment.[2] Babies need a suitably stimulating and playful environment where play and playing with available adults and other children is central.

For babies it is imperative that those who care for them in 'baby rooms' and nurseries share a sense of fun and joy and understand just how powerful babies' early play is in their overall development including their dispositions to learning, self-confidence, emotional stability and independence. While special toys are not necessary – babies will play with anything to hand, including things like keys and remote controls – baby toys, such as teddy bears, cloth books, rattles, mobiles, chewies and so on, in themselves can be interesting but all such experiences are enhanced by the presence of a caring, stimulating and playful play partner.

Babies grasp with their mouths and their hands and in so doing are exploring their immediate worlds – the beginnings of all other forms of play. Having someone playfully talk and sing to them enables sounds to be sorted in the baby's brain and gradually understood, including, and importantly, language. Through these sensory explorations, babies learn very quickly about themselves, other people, and the things and events in their surroundings. Babies learn about and react strongly to moods and tensions.[3] Sharing joy, laughter and fun with others promotes bonding and strengthens belonging and a sense of self. These early beginnings in play are the basis of empathy, compassion, trust and intimacy.

Example B1

Six-month-old Noah continually throws things on the floor from his high chair (like millions of other babies before him!) He enjoys the sound the cups, spoons and toys make on the floor. The playful reaction of his older brother in picking the things up and making faces when giving them back makes him laugh. He then drops a soft toy: it makes no noise. He looks surprised then peers over the edge of the chair. His brother, Joe, has quietly picked up the teddy and now holds it behind his back. Joe then makes it pop over Noah's shoulder much to his delight and tickles him with it: Noah takes it off him and drops it to the floor again with a big grin!

The play itself is interesting to the baby from an auditory perspective but the reaction of, and interaction with, his brother and the shared fun enable Noah to develop happy and loving relationships with a member of his immediate family. Other games such as peek-a-boo are not only fun but are therapeutic for babies, enabling them to understand the constancy of objects and that separation is not permanent.[4] Research into peek-a-boo games with 4-month-olds found that babies react significantly to different facial, emotional expressions with much more interest shown in happy/surprised faces.[5]

Photograph B1   Peek-a-boo game

As Tricia David maintains:

> Early in our lives, we are able to recognise playful, loving interactions with our most significant adults and older children and quickly participate in meaningful ways ... Our play becomes more complex as time goes on and as our understanding of the world in which we've found ourselves grows – if a baby is going to understand 'things' then they need to manipulate them, be it objects or, later, ideas. When we have grasped the fact that we are separate persons, with different likes and dislikes, we use that information to represent and invent aspects of that world, sometimes alone, but increasingly through fantasy play with other people who share our knowledge.[6]

Behaviours and play

Behaviours associated with play mean those characteristics of an experience that can signify 'play.' For example, eating one's dinner is not a play behaviour but piling up food on your plate and squashing it down are play behaviours! It is how it is expressed that makes some actions play and also who is involved.[7] Play is a process, a state of mind, like learning, the outward manifestation of which is an observable behaviour.[8]

'This is play' in children can be signified behaviourally in a number of ways as identified by several different researchers and writers over the last three decades:

- intrinsic motivation – play is for itself and what children do is more important than what they produce;
- playful frame of mind;
- children understand what they are doing in play, even though the adults may not!
- play generally energizes the players;
- play faces: among humans as well as some animals (e.g. apes), particular facial expressions (such as smiling) can denote a playful action or reaction rather than an aggressive one;[9]
- everything is possible be it real or imaginary: players are not bound by a particular mindset or approach;
- experimentation and active participation;
- mastery of skills and concepts;
- players choose the parameters of the play;
- children have confidence in play activities that has a positive effect on motivation, concentration and self-image;
- flexibility and creativity;

- trial and error learning;
- cultural expression;
- freely chosen/voluntary activity;
- enjoyable, fun, affective;
- no externally applied rules, although children make (and break!) 'rules' as they go along;
- positive effect on players (that said, play can be very serious and can involve children deeply);
- players' sense of ownership over the play.

A significant number of these characteristics need to be present for the behaviours to be classified as play. Many of these behaviours are identified by children when they define their own play behaviours.[10] Children tend to categorize their play behaviours as what you choose for yourself, something that does not involve adults, is voluntary, fun/enjoyable, and where the activity takes place (outdoors) usually represents play.[11] '...the important thing about play is not what it looks like but rather, what it means to approach a task as play.'[12] Of course, some of the above behaviours are also present in activities that might not be classified as play.[13]

Some play behaviours are, of course, risky; for example, where children challenge themselves to climb higher than they have climbed before or climb up the slide instead of sliding down.

Play behaviours often differ between boys and girls, particularly from the age of about 2-and-a-half years, with girls preferring to play using language – for example, role play and imitation – and boys preferring rough and tumble or other more energetic, physical behaviours.

Brain studies/neuroscience and play

It is known that children are born with more than 100 billion brain cells (neurons) that transmit nerve signals to and from the brain at up to 200 m.p.h. We will not grow any more neurons in our lifetimes. What will change is the connections made between them. Neurons consist of a cell body with branches (dendrites) that bring signals and a conductor for the nerve signal (an axon). At the end of the axon terminals transmit signals across a gap (the synapse) (see Diagram B1). A single cell can connect with as many as 15 000 other cells.[14]

Brain 'plasticity' means that the brain can change, adapt and grow from birth – changes occurring more rapidly in the first five years of life.[15] Plasticity prevents the brain from being static, enables new learning and is enhanced through stimulation. Stimulation is key to brain development and play is the

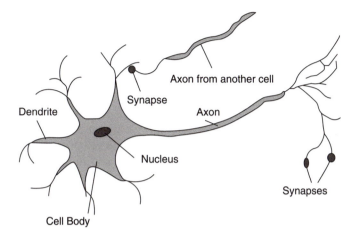

Diagram B1 Brain cells and connections[17]

fundamental stimulation for children (and adults). In fact, it has been shown that lack of play can have long-term effects that include physical harm (e.g. obesity), social harm (e.g. inability to share, negotiate, make friends), intellectual harm (e.g. less resilience to coping with pressures, lack of creativity) and emotional harm (e.g. not having fun and enjoying childhood).[16]

One study of 20 children reared in under-stimulating environments, with a lack of sensory and social play experiences in particular, were examined with sophisticated new brain-imaging techniques and other measures of brain growth. The children were found to have brains that were physically 20–30 per cent smaller than most children their age and, in over half the cases, parts of the children's brains appeared to have literally wasted away.[18]

The brain has two hemispheres – right and left – connected by nerve fibres. Most of us have a dominant side but this is flexible. Dominance from either hemisphere controls movement in the opposite side of the body. In general each hemisphere processes information in different ways but learning and thinking is more efficient when both sides of the brain work together. The left side of the brain processes information in a linear/sequential manner. The right brain processes from whole to parts. There appears to be little research that studies play from a neuroscience perspective (except in the field of language acquisition) but there are several websites where brain games are linked to accelerated learning (e.g. see www.acceleratedlearningmethods.com/right-brain-games.html). It is fair to speculate that 1) children who are right brain dominant will find jigsaw puzzles very challenging and 2) left brain dominant children may well be those who develop role-play 'narratives.'

Each child's brain is a powerful instrument: it is a complex, dynamic system and unique in its organization. How the brain develops is very much related to the environment the child experiences. Playful families and contexts are thought to produce more intelligent and flexibly thinking individuals. Children take more time to process information than adults and it is thought that this is why play exists as an innate behaviour. All brains respond to novelty and such originality often arises in playful contexts. In the early years much synaptic pruning happens 'so that older children actually have fewer but more interconnected neurons.'[19] Play enables children to absorb information in their own meaningful ways and in their own timescale: children play instinctively as a major part of their development.

Children's and adults' search for meaning is also innate: in their play children look for patterns, create perceptions, interact emotionally and challenge themselves without stress.[20] Children 'display high levels of motivation. Emotion, thought and action are in harmony – the dynamic system that is the brain in balance.'[21]

References

1. Gerhardt, S. (2004) *Why Love Matters: How Affection Shapes a Baby's Brain.* London: Routledge.
2. Gopnik, A. (2009) *The Philosophical Baby: What Children's Minds Tell Us About Truth, Love and the Meaning of Life.* London: Bodley Head.
3. Sunderland, M. (2007) *What Every Parents Needs to Know: The Incredible Effects of Love, Nurture and Play on Your Child's Development.* London: Dorling Kindersley.
4. Shore, R. (1997) *Rethinking the Brain: New Insights into Early Development.* New York: Families and Work Institute.
5. Montague, D. and Walker-Andrews, S. (2001) Peekaboo: a new look at infants' perception of emotion expressions, *Developmental Psychology*, 37(6): 826–38.
6. Tricia David (2011): personal communication.
7. Howard, J. (2010) The developmental and therapeutic potential of play: re-establishing teachers as play professionals. In J. Moyles (ed.) *The Excellence of Play* (3rd edn.). Maidenhead: Open University Press.
8. Smith, P.K. (2010) *Children and Play.* Chichester: Wiley-Blackwell.
9. See, for example, Jarvis, P. and George, J. (2010) Thinking it through: rough and tumble play. In J. Moyles (ed.) *Thinking About Play: Developing a Reflective Approach.* Maidenhead: Open University Press.
10. Garrick, R., Bath, C., Dunn, K., Maconochie, H., Willis, B. and Wolstenholme, C. (2011) *Children's Experiences of the Early Years Foundation Stage.* London: DfE Research Report DFE-RR071.
11. Howard, J. and McInnes, K. (2010) Thinking through the challenge of a play-based curriculum. In J. Moyles (ed.) *Thinking About Play: Developing a Reflective Approach.* Maidenhead: Open University Press.

12. Howard, J. and McInnes, K. (op. cit.).
13. Howard, J., Belling, W. and Rees, V. (2002) Eliciting children's perceptions of play and exploiting playfulness to maximise learning in the early years classroom. Paper presented at the BERA Conference, University of Exeter.
14. Brown, S. with Vaughan, C. (2010) *Play: How it Shapes the Brain, Opens the Imagination and Invigorates the Soul*. New York: Penguin.
15. Sprenger, M.B. (2008) *The Developing Brain: Birth to Age Eight*. Thousand Oaks, CA: Corwin Press.
16. Play England and the British Toy and Hobby Association (2011) *A World without Play*. Available online at www.maketime2play.co.uk/panelfindings.php (accessed 6 January 2012).
17. Taken from a diagram downloaded from the University of Nottingham site. Available online at www.cs.nott.ac.uk/~gxk/courses/g5aiai/006neuralnetworks/neural-networks.htm (accessed 6 January 2012).
18. Hawley, T. (2001) *Starting Smart: How Early Experiences Affect Brain Development* (3rd edn.). Washington, DC: Zero to Three: National Center for Infants, Toddlers and Families.
19. See Elkind, D. (2007) *The Power of Play: Learning What Comes Naturally*. Philadelphia: Da Capo Press (pp. 97–8 – example p. 99).
20. Pool, C.R. (1997) Maximizing learning: a conversation with Renate Nummela Caine, *Educational Leadership (How Children Learn)*, 54(6): 11–15.
21. Meade, A. (2001) One hundred billion neurons: how do they become organised? In T. David (ed.) *Promoting Evidence-based Practice in Early Childhood Education: Research and its Implications*. London: JAI/Elsevier Science.

C

Child-initiated play

Child-initiated play is thought to ensure children function with confidence and express their ideas. 'In doing this the child may make use of a variety of resources and demonstrate a complex range of knowledge, skills and understanding.'[1] Child-initiated play (and learning) stems from an English liberal tradition of valuing individual rights through a focus on independence and autonomy.[2] But it also has its basis in social-constructivist theories of learning.[3]

Child-initiated play is an activity, action or experience wholly decided upon by the child and is the result of the child's intrinsic motivation to explore, persevering for long periods of time and working at levels far higher than those sometimes identified in the planned curriculum. Such play experiences allow children increased ownership and responsibility in their experiences and learning. The HighScope Foundation reported that, in child-initiated play, children are more interpersonally interactive and have a greater variety of negotiation strategies. Children also showed 'the greatest mastery of basic reading, language and mathematics skills.'[4]

One study in Slovakia of pretend play in preschool children[5] found that in child-initiated role-play episodes:

- significantly more cognitive behaviours associated with thinking, knowing and remembering emerged;
- children's persistence and thinking behaviours increased;
- children took greater pleasure in play and learning.

The authors concluded that child-initiated play effectively supports children's problem-solving skills, social skills, literacy and mathematics. Child-initiated play activities rely on practitioners ensuring a plentiful supply and balance of open-ended resources.

'In child-initiated play the child is at the heart of decision-making: the experiences are often child-inspired, child-directed, child-led, child-managed and child-rich!'[6] In such situations it is the children's voices that are heard, at least in parallel, and frequently equally, with practitioners.

Within child-initiated playtime children are able to extend and apply their learning. They are free to explore, take risks, make decisions, solve problems and share their achievements with others. Children appear to apply the knowledge and skills they gain from other areas of learning in a meaningful context. They consolidate and internalize, thus forming deeper understandings.

Example C1

The children had been on a visit to the seaside and were encouraged to create 'the beach' as a role-play area in the corner of the classroom including sand, water, windbreak, etc. Some of the additional resources were stored in boxes so that children could create their own beach setting. Two children decided to make sandcastles and found shells in a labelled container and decorated their castles, counting and describing as they played.

The play in Example C1 was child-initiated, support from the educators coming through encouragement and the resources subtly provided, initially the materials to recreate the beach and, later, the materials for sandcastles and decoration.

The educators' roles in child-initiated learning are complex: mainly, adults observe and record how, through children's own agency, they are able to play and organize their learning including social dimensions of play and resources, learning in the process about individual children's knowledge, skills and understanding. They allow at least half of each day to children's own initiated play and learning experiences. Educators record the events inherent in child-initiated play so that they are able, at a future time, to provide resources and/or support that could potentially extend or enhance the child-initiated play. Talking to the children once the child-initiated play has run its course – plus the observations – will enable educators to learn about children's experiences and learning during the child-initiated period and will allow children a voice in their own learning.

Sandra Smidt affirms

> ... by encouraging children to follow their own interests we help them become critical, thoughtful and potentially transformative adults. The kind of education I want to see is one which promotes questioning and creativity, rather than repetition and conformity ... I would advocate ... a 'playful pedagogy' that encourages learners to be and remain critical and creative in their thinking, their approach to learning and their analysis of the world they inhabit.[7]

Cognitive play and learning and metacognition

Cognition is the study of 'knowing' (this section should be read in conjunction with B = Brain). Cognitive learning is extremely powerful: it provides the means of knowledge and understanding. It emerges through the senses – listening, touching, watching, smelling, moving and experiencing things for oneself – and this, in turn, develops memory, reasoning and problem-solving abilities. Metacognition/metacognitive learning is about understanding one's own thinking processes and how one comes to 'know' and 'understand': it necessitates reflection. Through these actions, we come to process and remember what we have *directly experienced* that makes sense to us and facilitates greater numbers of connections in the brain. For children, therefore, play and first-hand experience is the most central means of both cognitive and metacognitive learning, although the latter takes much longer to develop.[8] The brain has been shown to be extremely active during play and playful encounters. Most children's learning potential is limitless: only their lack of experience and accumulated knowledge limits their abilities. It is through play that children acquire this experience and actively construct patterns identified and learned through play to make sense of the new experience or absorb the new information.

When children play together they gain an understanding of others' thoughts and feelings and learn to see things from others' points of view:

this process is known as 'theory of mind' and is extremely important in understanding other children's intentions, needs and beliefs, and interacting effectively with them socially.[9] Empathy is a related concept. Pretend play is thought to contribute greatly to cognitive development in children as it 'requires the ability to transform objects and actions symbolically; it is furthered by interactive social dialogue and negotiation; and it involves role taking, script knowledge, and improvisation.'[10] Children as young as 2-years-old can talk about what they want, like and feel; when they are 3, they also talk about what other people think and know.[11]

Constructivism (the Piagetian view of learning; that is, children construct their own meaning) has been superseded by the Vygotskian notion of social constructivism; that is, children learn through interaction with others in a social context from their 'zone of proximal development' (their current level of understanding).[12] Social constructivism is the basis of holistic and non-linear learning approaches in, for example, Scandinavian countries, the *Reggio Emilia* preschools in Italy and *Te Whāriki* in New Zealand and

> is based upon a common desire to establish early learning [playful] experiences for young children which encourage lifelong values ... in tandem with a commitment to the rights of the individual, as well as the development of critical thinking abilities.[13]

Within such play-based approaches children learn self-regulation (see I = Independence) and with the help of experienced educators (including parents and older peers) children choose, organize and reflect metacognitively on their own meaningful and relevant experiences.[14] In these approaches, learning is redefined – children do not need to be 'taught' as such but learning occurs in the context of children's development of 'executive functions.' Executive function is a critical cognitive skill and a growing area of neuroscience and psychology research. Beginning in babies and developing through into adulthood, it involves learning the skills of planning, organizing, setting goals, having a working memory, being flexible and paying attention to detail in order to achieve goals.

Example C2

Archie, aged 5 months, is avidly watching a mobile above his cot. He accidently kicks his legs out and the mobile spins and plays music. Another involuntary kick and it happens again. Quickly, Archie recognizes the cause and effect relationship and kicks his legs out over and over again showing the beginnings of executive functioning.

'To be successful takes creativity, flexibility, self-control and discipline. Central to all those are executive functions, including mentally playing with ideas, giving a considered rather than an impulsive response, and staying focused.'[15] Play, games and physical activities are all known to support the development of executive functions alongside emotional and social development and experiences that involve challenge.

Photograph C1   Playful learning

Playful learning experiences, particularly those that involve children in planning, executing and evaluating their own activities, support the development of executive functioning. Some behavioural problems are thought to be associated with executive function deficit.

Consumerism/commercialism and play

Consumerism, commercialization and marketing affect every aspect of children's lives today, frequently dictating how they play and learn and what, for example, they eat. This consumerism has, according to many, become a barrier to a good childhood and quality play experiences.[16] One aspect of this is the increase of obesity in young children because of (1) the sedentary nature of activities such as television watching, computers and electronic games,[17] and (2) the marketing of junk foods to children and parents. There has also been a steady decline over recent years in the opportunities children have for physical outdoor play because of fears from parents about potential risks from traffic, strangers and even older children. 'The most high-profile health issue is the dramatic rise in childhood obesity. . . . Obesity in children under 11 has risen by over 40% in ten years.'[18]

Commercialization means that old established play behaviours, like dressing up, have become something of a fashion parade, rather than the taking on of different roles and emotions, which is not only fun but generates much activity and thinking for children. Dressing up has taken on different connotations thanks to commercialism and many are concerned about the sexualization of very young children's play. Young children have a 'natural, healthy interest in their sexuality. But when their developing sexuality is moulded to fit adult sexual stereotypes, this can compromise that healthy developmental process.'[19] 'Selling adult fashion trends to children inevitably leads to the premature sexualisation of little girls, with five- and six-year-olds arriving at schools in sexy thongs and lacy bras.'[20]

From a play point of view, there always seems to have been major advertising of toys – well, at least since there's been radio, television and shops! The difference in the twenty-first century is that the production of such toys – and children's creativity and flexibility in playing with them – has changed significantly. Many toys now are developed as a result of television, cinema and computer programs (such as Star Wars, Barbie, My Little Pony, Dr Who) and have lost much of their creativity in use, rendering play something different from the free choice, flexible process it is known to be (see B = Behaviours and play). It may seem that children have play choices just as they always did but this is a choice from only those things that parents, peer pressure and the media determine for even very young children.[21] Designer children's wear and toys are common (even for babies and even if one cannot afford it) yet there is much research to show that 'old-fashioned' play – that is, playing outdoors, imaginative games with one's friends – provide children with many more opportunities for playful learning experiences leading to executive functioning of the brain[22] (see C = Cognitive play and learning and metacognition).

Arguably, computers, tablets, Xboxes and other technological 'toys' bring a different kind of play and learning:[23] '. . . the commercial world could be seen to offer children many opportunities in terms of entertainment, creativity, communication, learning and cultural experience that they would not otherwise have. However, the benefits of this are hard to separate out and to quantify.'[24] It is easy to predict, however, that electronic toys are likely to have the effect of making children sedentary and lacking many social skills. Such toys are thought to shrink the size of children's imaginative space[25] and 'instil the psychology of consumerism as much or more than they serve the inculcation of manners, morals and social roles.'[26] Young children, in particular, 'need a real rather than a virtual reality'[27] if they are to thrive and be happy, balanced human beings. Further, children's electronic toys remove any opportunity children might have for understanding how things 'work' in the way they could when toys could be taken apart and reconstructed as well as moving them away from the natural world and outdoor play.[28]

> For boys especially, commercial companies concentrate on nurturing the competitive instinct and appealing to their inbuilt desires for power, force, mastery, domination and control as well as their natural interest in gadgets and technology. The massive computer games industry is testament to this.[29]

There are also significant concerns about what many see as harmful impacts on children's well-being, especially on their mental and physical health.[30] That said, there is no doubt that children for the last two or more decades have been the target of commercial organizations and that their play has been influenced significantly by this move – whether for good or ill, time and research may tell. But it is also clear that children are brainwashed into wanting the latest plaything even if it is extremely disappointing once acquired!

Example C3

Four-year-old Marty desperately wanted an electronic i-Helicopter for his birthday because his friend had one. It looked very exciting as it flew up in the air under his friend's control and landed on the floor. Sure enough, when the day arrived, Marty duly received his helicopter. While he opened his other presents, his mum got it working for him and he watched as she manipulated the machine. He then had a go himself and for all of 3–4 minutes he was interested in manoeuvring it. Then he spotted the box (a big one) and the packaging still on the floor. He and his brother spent the next 45 minutes using the box and packaging in all sorts of imaginative ways to develop a story about 'baddies' in prison!

Evidence suggests that all this consumerism has not made children any happier or more fulfilled in life, despite their assertion that 'I must have THAT because *everybody's* got one!' In a recent UNICEF survey about children's well-being, British children emerged in the bottom third of developed countries on measures such as happiness and came out worst in relation to family and peer relationships.[31] The old saying: 'Those who play together, stay together' seems apt here at a time when families with young children are often too busy working and 'consuming' goods and services to give quality play time to their children.'[32]

David Whitebread and Sue Bingham[33] are clear:

> 'There are rafts of research showing that happiness doesn't come from having more stuff. It comes from having friends, family and social interaction, from the feeling that there's more to life than mere self-gratification, and from spending time doing something you personally think worthwhile' such as, of course, playing together. Sue Palmer believes large numbers of 'very young children have played games like Mortal Kombat and Grand Theft Auto III (rated 18+). Often unsuspecting parents buy computer games with high age ratings for their children because their friends have it.'[34]

Consumerism and commercialism affect the very culture of children's play.

Creativity and play

Play is in itself a creative act and process, as we have seen elsewhere, because it releases the inhibitions that are thought to restrict creativity, which is the freest form of self-expression.[35] Creativity means bringing something of yourself to everything you do, just as children do in play. Play is also recreation – quite literally: play allows one to create and recreate the world through one's own senses and feelings in a relaxed and pleasurable way. The freedom to play stimulates the creative imagination[36] as it arouses curiosity, enables us to think without boundaries and discover novelty, try out new things without fear of failure, imagine and adapt our ideas. All these are both the basis of learning and related to executive function in the brain.

Creativity goes beyond 'the arts' for children though they have a big part in developing symbolic thought. Creativity is the very basis of their actions and thinking. Children want to try out new things in new ways with the approval of adults. Unfortunately for practitioners some of the most creative children are also the most challenging emotionally and behaviourally!

The best inventions and artistic works often come from trial and error and being prepared to learn from mistakes. Originality is also characteristic of creativity and, together with trial and error learning, is a major attribute of play. Creativity is an intellectual process and as children are usually 'full' of creativity (when allowed to be), this indicates the strong link between the brain and creativity. But creativity is also an affective, emotional process – without caring enough about something to pursue it, new ideas would not be uncovered nor art produced. Art is a novel way of looking at the world and, because of their relative inexperience, children inevitably view the world differently from adults: therefore, we cannot 'judge' children's creative outcomes with adult values.

Photograph C2   Being creative outdoors

Creativity is the basis of all human advancement: where would we be without the creative genius of the likes of Einstein or Newton who have helped us to understand our world or Leonardo da Vinci or the wonderful works of art created by the likes of, for example, Renoir, Monet and their contemporaries? Picasso (1881–1973) insisted on the importance of retaining a child-like approach to his art: 'All children are artists. The problem is how to remain an artist once he grows up' and 'It took me four years to paint like Raphael, but a lifetime to paint like a child.'[37]

To sum up, anyone can be creative in an everyday and even specialist aesthetic way, but not everyone can be world-shatteringly creative! Being creative requires creative thinking and practitioners who can 'incubate' children's creativity and develop it.[38] As Fisher proposes: 'The world, as it is presented to us, is not the only possible world.'[39] Being creative allows children to see other possibilities.

Culture and play

Culture is a term that encompasses a range of different aspects of life: excellence in taste (high culture), the integrated patterns of knowledge, belief and behaviour that influence our capacity for symbolic thought and social learning and, perhaps most importantly, the set of attitudes, values, goals and practices that we share with others (traditional culture). Culture is also a form of action – with children, this action is play that forms a major component of children's culture: the culture of childhood. The culture of the 'worlds' children inhabit – such as their play worlds and institutional cultures like settings, schools, homes – have specific qualities and are worthy of study as they directly influence children's development and learning. '. . . as play grows more complex . . . it becomes a distinct world that players seek to revisit. Traditions emerge and play itself acquires characteristics that are ritual-like.'[40]

Some researchers feel strongly that children are 'agents' existing primarily within their own peer cultures, whose own understandings, symbols, rituals and other meaning systems are sufficiently potent to significantly influence broader social phenomena such as social change, family life, and education.[41] Children's play serves as an enculturating mechanism[42] and is an essential aspect of children's culture and quality of life. Children's play is an initiation into a wider cultural circle and leads to building friendships and generating understanding of others' actions and reactions. The media culture, now prevalent in children's lives, has already been briefly mentioned above and we have seen that consumerism is part of children's culture whether we like it or not!

Kalliala believes children 'have the right to their own [cultural] experiences. They have the right to be interested in matters that adults do not find interesting.'[43] Freedom to play is part of that right. The culture of the setting or school will significantly influence children's cultural worlds in relation to how much freedom and choice children are given and how far they are encouraged towards self-regulation/independence. Play also influences their role as future citizens: 'Play promotes attributes essential to a democratic populace, such as curiosity, reasoning, empathy, sharing, cooperation and a sense of competence – a belief that the individual can make a difference to the world.'[44]

Children's culture is changing dramatically at the present time not just down to commercialism and changes in the types of 'toys' that they use but because of the social, political, economic and cultural changes through the whole of society[45] which are affecting children's lives, such as poverty or health.

A universal element across all cultures is children's play and play can act as a means of promoting cultural/multicultural awareness in young children. We know that some time between ages 3 and 4 years children become aware of differences based on racial and ethnic background.[46] Ensuring young children develop appropriate attitudes is one of the practitioner's roles: cultural diversity in children's play means practitioners ensuring that a range of cultures are always represented in the setting/school and that cultural values and norms are discussed and respected and that early educators work to ensure positive awareness of individual differences, ethnic identities and cultural diversity in playful and meaningful ways.[47]

Liz Brooker concludes

> ... in many communities children's play is understood as beneficial for their development and learning ... the apparently universal appreciation of 'pretend play' as a preparation for adult life, and a space to try out cultural behaviours, suggests that parents everywhere are able to identify a role for play in preparing children for participation in the culture, if not for teaching them school-like knowledge and skills.[48]

Curriculum and play

'There is, then, abundant evidence that play-based programs [curricula] are at least as supportive (or more supportive) of academic achievement as are didactic programs. And they carry much less risk of creating anxiety and low self-esteem.'[49] This section is not about individual subjects but about the early years curriculum as a whole, which could be said to be all the things a child experiences which promote learning in its many forms – social, emotional, intellectual, moral, physical, creative – in fact all those forms that are more than subjects.

Play is not a break from the curriculum; play is the best way to implement the curriculum.[50] Much of a child's learning experiences will be informal (e.g. learning at home and outside) but in accountability-based systems young children's learning will be in formal systems such as schools and settings all of which will have some form of implemented curriculum, be it one on which policy makers have decided (like the *Early Years Foundation Stage* in England) or one developed through a particular philosophy like the Waldorf Steiner Schools. Some countries (as we have seen in section B) have curricula based on children's holistic development and a belief in individuals as competent, capable learners in their own right who are fully functioning young members of society. England is one of only a very few countries where formal curricular learning can start as early as 4-years-old.

In its broadest sense, the curriculum also encompasses both affective and physical environments for young children and places equal value on care and learning, as well as provision for space and time to play and grow. The most effective curricula are play-based and recognize the interests, experiences and choices of children; they are process-related and support the development of skills and positive dispositions to learning. '*Playful learning* offers one way to reframe the debate by nesting a rich core curriculum within a playful pedagogy.'[51] Curricula leaders must also reflect on all these aspects of children's education and care[52] in order to ensure that the curriculum meets the children's needs and is suitably play-based and playful. Where 'subjects' or 'themes' are part of the designated curriculum, for all children under 6-years-old they should be implemented through play. Children can readily be engaged in playing physically and socially and learning about language and literacy, mathematics, and their immediate environment and community. Research has shown, for example, that preschool children engage in more talk and activities relating to mathematical concepts when number symbols are embedded in play settings[53] and when children are allowed free access to make their own symbolic meanings.[54]

Example C4 (from curriculum and play research[55])

Hirsh-Pasek and colleagues experimented with three ways of teaching children about shapes. In one, the children simply played with the shapes. In the second, the children were taught didactically about shapes (naming them, e.g. this is a square) and in the third, children were allowed to explore but the teacher stepped in and asked questions: 'How are these two shapes the same? How are they different?' They found that children learn the most about shapes when they are able to explore and are asked open-ended questions that extend thinking.

References

1. Qualifications and Curriculum Authority (2008) *Early Years Foundation Stage Profile Handbook*. London: QCA.
2. Kwon, Y.-I. (2003) A comparative analysis of preschool education in Korea and England, *Comparative Education*, 39(4): 479–91.
3. Vygotsky, L. (1978) *Mind in Society: The Development of Higher Psychological Processes*. Cambridge, MA: Harvard University Press.
   See also Rogoff, B. (1998) Cognition as a collaborative process. In D. Kuhn and R.S. Siegler (eds) *Handbook of Child Psychology, Vol. 2: Cognition, Perception and Language* (5th edn.). New York: John Wiley.
4. Schweinhart, L. (1997) *Child-initiated Learning Activities for Young Children Living in Poverty*. CEEP Archive of ERIC/EECE Digests. Available online at www.ceep.crc.uiuc.edu/eecearchive/digests/1997/schwei97.html.
5. Gmitrova, V. and Gmitrova, G. (2003) The impact of teacher-directed and child-directed pretend play on cognitive competence in kindergarten children, *Early Childhood Education Journal*, 30(4): 241–46.

6. Moyles, J. (2008) Empowering children and adults: play and child-initiated learning. In S. Featherstone and P. Featherstone (eds) *Like Bees not Butterflies*. London: A&C Black (p. 32).

7. Sandra Smidt (2011): personal communication.

8. Goswami, U. and Bryan, P. (2007) *Children's Cognitive Development and Learning. Primary Review Research Briefings 2/1a*. Cambridge: University of Cambridge.

9. Astington, J. and Edward, M. (2010) *The Development of Theory of Mind in Early Childhood: Encyclopaedia on Early Childhood Development*. Available online at www.child-encyclopedia.com/documents/Astington-EdwardANGxp.pdf (accessed 10 January 2012).

10. Bergen, D. (2001) The role of pretend play in children's cognitive development, *Early Childhood Research and Practice*, 4(1). Available online at www.ecrp.uiuc.edu/v4n1/bergen.html (accessed 7 January 2012).

11. Bartsch, K. and Wellman, H. (1995) *Children Talk About the Mind*. New York: Oxford University Press.

12. Vygotsky, L. (op. cit.)

13. Whitebread, D. and Bingham S. (2012) School readiness: a critical review of perspectives and evidence. Draft document commissioned by TACTYC: Association of the Professional Development of Early Years Educators Available online at www.tactyc.org.uk. (p. 35).

14. Alvestad, M. and Duncan, J. (2001) 'The value is enormous – It's priceless I think!' New Zealand preschool teachers' understanding of the early childhood curriculum in New Zealand – a comparative perspective, *International Journal of Early Childhood*, 38(1): 31–45.

15. Diamond, A. and Lee, K. (2011) Interventions shown to aid executive function development in children 4–12 years old, *Science*, 333(6045): 959–64.

16. Palmer, S. (2007) *Toxic Childhood: How the Modern World is Damaging our Children and What We Can Do About It*. London: Orion.

17. Livingstone, S. (2006) Does TV advertising make children fat? What the evidence tells us, *Public Policy Research,* 13(1): 54–61.

18. The Stationery Office (2004, 2006) *Health Survey for England*. London: TSO.

19. Papadopoulos, L. (2010) *Sexualisation of Young People Review*. London: Home Office. Available online at www.drlinda.co.uk/pdfs/sexualisation_review.pdf (accessed 12 January 2012).

20. Sue Palmer, personal communication with author.

21. Letting Children be Children: Report of an Independent Review of the Commercialisation and Sexualisation of Childhood (2011) London: Department for Education (DfE).

22. Chudacoff, H. (2008) *Children at Play: An American History*. New York: New York University Press.

23. Pellegrini, A. (2009) *The Role of Play in Human Development*. New York and Oxford: Oxford University Press.

24. Department for Children, Schools and Families (DCSF) (2009) *The Impact of the Commercial World on Children's Wellbeing: Report of an Independent Assessment*. Nottingham: DCSF (para 19). Available online at www.education. gov.uk/publications/standard/publicationDetail/Page1/DCSF-00669-2009 (accessed 10 January 2012). *See also* Department for Education (DfE) (2011) *Letting Children be Children: An Independent Review of the Commercialisation and Sexualisation of Childhood (the Bailey Report)*. London: DfE.
25. Chudacoff (op. cit.)
26. Elkind, D. (2007) *The Power of Play*. Philadelphia, PA: Da Capo Press (p. 24).
27. Oldfield, L. (2011) The Steiner Waldorf Foundation Stage – 'To everything there is a season.' In R. House (ed.) *Too Much, Too Soon? Early Learning and the Erosion of Childhood*. Stroud: Hawthorn Press.
28. Elkind (op. cit.: p. 22).
29. COMPASS (2007) *Commercialisation of Childhood*. London: Compass (p. 12).
30. COMPASS (ibid.).
31. United Nations Children's Fund (2007) *An Overview of Child Well-being in Rich Countries*. Florence: UNICEF.
32. UNICEF (ibid.).
33. Whitebread, D. and Bingham S. (op. cit.)
34. Palmer, S. (op. cit.)
35. Craft, A. (2002) *Creativity in the Early Years*. London: Continuum.
36. Duffy, B. (2006) *Supporting Creativity and Imagination in the Early Years* (2nd edn.). Maidenhead: Open University Press.
37. Picasso, P. (1881–1973) Quotation source available online at www. thinkexist.com (accessed 15 January 2012).
38. Bruce, T. (2011) *Cultivating Creativity: For Babies, Toddlers and Young Children*. London: Hodder.
39. Fisher, R. (2005) What is creativity? In R. Fisher and M. Williams (eds) *Unlocking Creativity: Teaching Across the Curriculum*. London: David Fulton (p. 11).
40. Masters, P. (2008) Play theory, playing and culture, *Sociology Compass*, 2/3: 856–69 (p. 858).
41. Corsaro, S.A. (2004) *The Sociology of Childhood* (2nd edn.). Thousand Oaks, CA: Pine Forge Press.
42. Schwartzman, H. (1978) *Transformations: The Anthropology of Children's Play*. New York: Plenum Press.
43. Kalliala, M. (2005) *Play Culture in a Changing World*. Maidenhead: Open University Press (p. 4).
44. Linn, S. (2010) Commercialism in children's lives. In *2010 State of the World: From Consumerism to Sustainability*. New York: WorldWatch Institute/W.W. Norton (p. 62)
45. Lego Learning Institute (2003) *The Changing Face of Children's Play Culture*. Slough: The Lego Learning Institute.

46. Hirschfeld, L.A. (2008) Children's developing conceptions of race. In S.M. Quintana and C. McKown (eds) *Handbook of Race, Racism, and the Developing Child*. Hoboken, NJ: John Wiley & Sons, Inc.

47. Ramsey, P.G. (2004) *Teaching and Learning in a Diverse World: Multicultural Education for Young Children*. New York: Teachers' College Press.

48. Elizabeth Brooker, personal communication with author.

49. Elkind (op. cit.: p. 212).

50. Tepperman, J. (ed.) (2007) *Play in the Early Years: Key to School Success*. Oakland, CA: Early Childhood Funders. Available online at www.4children.org/images/pdf/play07.pdf (accessed 5 February 2012).

51. Hirsh-Pasek, K. and Golinkoff, R. (2011) The great balancing act: optimizing core curricula through playful pedagogy. In E. Zigler, S. Barnett and W. Gilliam (eds) *The Preschool Education Debates*. Baltimore, MD: Paul H. Brookes Publishing Company.

52. Curtis, D. and Carter, M. (2007) *Learning Together with Young Children: A Curricular Framework for Reflective Teachers*. St Pauls, MN: Redleaf Press.

53. Cook, D. (2000) Voice practice: social and mathematical talk in imaginative play, *Early Child Development and Care*, 162: 51–63.

54. Worthington, M. and Carruthers, E. (2011) *Understanding Children's Mathematical Graphics: Beginning in Play*. Maidenhead: Open University Press.

55. Fisher, K., Nash, B., Hirsh-Pasek, K., Newcombe, N. and Golinkoff, R. (2009) Breaking the mold: altering preschoolers' concepts of geometric shapes. Poster presented at the biennial Society for Research in Child Development, Denver, Colorado, April.

D

Decision-making and play
Deep-level learning and play
Definitions of play (given throughout the book)
Dispositions to play and learning

Decision-making and play

In play, children frequently show themselves to be effective decision makers: whether to put another block on the top of that already wobbly tower or pour just one more cup of water into that container. They then, like the rest of us, have to live with the consequences of the decision they have made and, hopefully, learn something for next time. In this sense, children are agents in their own learning, which is a key factor of effective decision making.[1] This process also means that they are researchers of their own play processes and outcomes and learn skills and dispositions transferable to other contexts, particularly if they have a supportive 'other' who helps them think through cause and effect and problem solving.

It is somewhat surprising, then, that only recently has it been felt that children could be involved in making other decisions about their lives and their play; for example, what is needed in play spaces specifically designated for young children. The children's right to play[2] and to be part of decisions about that play is already enshrined in law. The giving of a voice to children is very much embedded in current policy initiatives such as Sheffkids[3] and is part of the empowering of children:[4] the belief is that giving children responsibility will enhance their sense of self-identity, belonging and usefulness.

'When children and young people have the opportunity to identify the problems that affect their lives and, most importantly, find and implement the solutions, it builds their self-confidence and encourages them to value the positive impact they can have on the lives of others.'[5] Involving young children as researchers of their own play and learning experiences has not been common but is an increasingly recommended practice. Children as *researchers* is a very different concept from children as *subjects* of research.[6] Researchers have interviewed young children (e.g. to ask them about what they define as play in schools[7]) but children can also investigate for themselves, for example, about which play experiences are most useful and enjoyable.

Having researched play with and by children, the next stage is to involve children in the design of new playful learning experiences in collaboration with their peers. This can lead to policy changes in schools. Children can be encouraged to take photographs of play activities and then analyse these to decide what they are learning. However, it is generally agreed that children are insufficiently involved in such activities

> in spite of the fact that just over half of our sample of organisations surveyed were responsible for developing services and policies that would affect children under eight, and that the majority of adult survey respondents (in both surveys) 'agreed' or 'strongly agreed' that there were no decisions children could not be involved in, provided they were properly supported.[8]

Of course, this means a sharing of power between children and adults and differential power relationships that have not been traditional practice in most schools and settings.

Deep-level learning and play

Play is central to deep-level learning based, as it is, upon the constructivist and social-constructivist traditions; that is, children constructing and making meaning from hands-on, experiential learning and with the support of someone more expert. Real learning (play in this case) affects deeper cognitive processing on which competences and dispositions are built. Deep-level processing focuses on underlying meanings and requires the learner's personal commitment to understanding and applying knowledge to real-life situations. It also requires the learner to reflect on the links between different pieces of information and synthesize this information with their prior learning. (The opposite – surface or superficial level learning – is related to rote learning and simple memorization.) Table D1 summarizes what deep and surface pedagogy might look like from a play perspective.

Deep-level learning is often sustained over long periods of time. In the *Researching Effective Pedagogy in the Early Years (REPEY)* project, the researchers found that preschool children do best when they are engaged in activities which are sustained over time and which make them think deeply; particularly, 'environments that encourage "sustained shared thinking" between adults and children make more cognitive, linguistic and social behavioural progress',[9] some of these recognized in play contexts. This latter research

Table D1 Learning through play and deep/surface structures

Playful pedagogy through deep and surface structures	
Deep approaches	*Surface approaches*
Practitioner demonstrates commitment and enthusiasm to children's play and exhibits playfulness	Practitioner is only concerned with what she wants to 'teach'
Practitioner demonstrates an interest and involvement in the children's learning through play	Practitioner does not understand children's learning through play
Learning intentions in play experiences are clearly understood and conveyed to children sensitively	Conflicting messages are given by practitioner's actions in terms of the value of play (e.g. 'You can play after you've finished your work')
Meaningfulness to the child of the play/playful activities is stressed	Little feedback is given to the children on their skills and understandings developed through play
Practitioner fosters children's engagement with their own learning through play	Assessment methods emphasize memory and recall – a check-list mentality!
Children are given choice and opportunity to exercise self-regulation in their play and learning experiences	Few opportunities are given for independence or self-regulation – play is continually adult-directed
Children are encouraged to analyse and evaluate their own learning through play and understand how these build on previous experiences	Children are familiarized with surface approaches from previous experiences and are not encouraged to think more deeply about their play and learning

has stressed the link between SST and deeper levels of learning for children through their co-construction of play with other children or adults.

Deep-level learning should not be underestimated: children must be 'involved:'[10] this is where play and its motivational and committed elements becomes vital. Using the components of deep learning identified by Ramsden (in brackets),[11] the example (D1) shows a play episode involving deep learning.

Example D1

Following a visit to the local library, a group of 6-year-olds ask if they can make a class library (*understanding the structure of a task, in this case, self-determined*). They have problems with the classification of the books and are asked what they remember of how books were classified in the library (*relate previous knowledge to new knowledge*). The photographs that children took at the library are used to remind them of their previous experience and understanding, and several children draw plans of what their library should look like (*relate knowledge from other subjects*). Discussion ensues about which books should be put where on the shelving (*relate evidence – from photographs and drawings – and argument*). When the library is finally formed to the children's satisfaction (*organization into a coherent whole*), the children analyse and evaluate what they have learned and how the library 'works,' deciding on relevant changes (*emphasis on internal understanding and meaning*) such as the need for the computer in this area.

Dispositions to play and learning

The word 'disposition' has many different meanings, but in this context it is about children's learning dispositions and the role of play in forming them. 'Dispositions are frequent and voluntary habits of thinking and doing.'[12] While play is, as we have seen, innate, dispositions – ways of approaching tasks and activities – are learned through a wide range of experiences in a variety of contexts. We can learn a disposition towards friendliness or selfishness! Dispositions can be positive or negative. The majority are learned in childhood through play.

The disposition to do or learn something can be readily exemplified for practitioners: just think of the child who may well develop skills for reading, such as phonics, but does not have the disposition (the frame of mind or attitude) to read for pleasure. Without positive dispositions, children may learn a wide range of skills and acquire a great deal of knowledge, but may choose not to apply these. Having a positive approach – or disposition – to learning is felt to be a major factor contributing to children's progress in settings and schools. Dispositions regulate how we play and learn well beyond our early childhood years: this is why the promotion of positive learning dispositions is inbuilt into the *Te Whāriki* curriculum.[13]

It is clear that play-based curricula promote many positive dispositions, including curiosity, persistence, concentration, perseverance, helpfulness, 'stickability,' altruism and the taking on of responsibility. Learning dispositions have three forms: academic, such as the ability to gather bits of information; intellectual, such as the ability to analyse, theorize, ask questions and solve problems, and to be curious and be creative; social, for example co-operation and self-regulation.

Photograph D1   Developing a disposition to explore and learn

Lilian Katz suggests that practitioners should strengthen intellectual dispositions by asking open-ended, thought-provoking questions and modelling other dispositions they want to promote in children such as curiosity[14] and, of course, playfulness and humour. She suggests that 'The early introduction of formal instruction often causes children to behave as though they understand something, when in fact they do not. In this way, their confidence in their own intellect may be undermined very early on', resulting in children doubting their own skills and abilities.[15]

'Playfulness is one of the most important dispositions to support children's learning'[16] and is both innate and learned. Playfulness imbues children with further dispositions towards imagination, collaboration, exploration, observation, independence and self-management, spontaneity, sensitivity to others, creativity, risk-taking and social competence, among others. It is vital that practitioners sponsor children's innate playfulness if they are to enable children to develop appropriate intellectual dispositions. 'Effective early childhood teachers consider whether their behaviors empower or undermine children's dispositions, then alter their practices accordingly.'[17]

Example D2

Joe is playing in the sand tray, totally absorbed in filling a range of containers and is unaware of anything and anyone around him. He fetches and fills more containers until the whole sand tray has no more space for them – and no more sand. Joe's dispositions to concentrate, persist, explore, observe and self-manage are evident. And all the practitioner has done is supply materials!

References

1. Children in Scotland (2009) *The Child as Protagonist: Working with the Child as Agents in their own Development and Learning*. Available online at www.childreninscotland.org.uk (accessed 25 February 2012).
2. UNICEF (1989) *United Nations Convention on the Rights of the Child*. Available online at www.unicef.org/crc (accessed 3 March 2012).
3. See, for example, Sheffkids at www.sheffkids.co.uk/childrenssite/pages/haveyoursay.html.
4. Young Children's Voices Network, National Children's Bureau at www.ncb.org.uk/media/60340/ycvn_evaluation_report.pdf.
5. Children's Rights Alliance for England (2010) *Children's Participation in Decision-making: A Summary Report on Progress Made up to 2010*. London: Participation Works (p. 9). Available online at www.participationworks.org.uk/files/webfm/files/npf~/npf_publications/A%20Summary%20Report_jun10.pdf (accessed 9 January 2012).
6. Kellett, M. (2010) *Rethinking Children and Research: Attitudes in Contemporary Society*. London: Continuum.
7. Clark, A. (2005) Listening to and involving young children: a review of research and practice, *Early Child Development and Care*, 175(6): 489–505.
8. Children's Rights Alliance for England (op. cit.)
9. Siraj-Blatchford, I., Muttock, S., Sylva, K., Gilden, R. and Bell, D. (2002) *Researching Effective Pedagogy in the Early Years (REPEY)*. London: Department of Educational Studies (DES).
10. Laevers, F. (1993) Deep level learning: an exemplary application on the area of physical knowledge, *European Early Childhood Education Research Journal*, 1(1): 53–68 (EJ 467 556).
11. Ramsden, P. (1992) *Learning to Teach in Higher Education*. London: Routledge (p. 46).
12. Ros-Voseles, D. and Fowler-Haughey, S. (2007) *Why Children's Disposition Should Matter to All Teachers*. NAEYC Beyond the Journal: Young Children on the Web. Available online at www.naeyc.org/files/yc/file/200709/DaRos-Voseles.pdf (accessed 26 February 2012).
13. New Zealand Ministry of Education (1996) *Te Whāriki Early Childhood Curriculum*. Wellington: New Zealand.
14. Cited in Ros-Voseles, D. and Fowler-Haughey, S. (op. cit.) (p. 1).
15. Katz, L. (2011) Endpiece: where are we now and where should we be going? In T. Papatheodorou and J. Moyles (eds) *Cross-Cultural Perspectives on Early Childhood*. London: Sage Publications (p. 220).
16. Thomas, F. and Harding, S. (2011) The role of play: play outdoors as the medium and mechanism for well-being, learning and development. In J. White (ed.) *Outdoor Provision in the Early Years*. London: Paul Chapman (pp. 13–14).
17. Ros-Voseles, D. and Fowler-Haughey, S. (op. cit.) (p. 7).

E

Emotional development and play

Emotional development is often subsumed under social development and, while there is no denying that emotionally stable children are often more sociable children, it has a separate section given the growing importance shown by much contemporary research of emotional learning. Self-awareness, self-management, social awareness, relationship management and flexibility are all aspects of emotional development, and to acquire these we need to engage the emotional part of the brain through our senses. The key period for emotional development is from birth to 12-years-old: play is, therefore, thought to be children's innate way of providing simultaneously for emotional and intellectual development in this period.[1]

Psychologist Daniel Goleman emphasizes the vital importance of what he calls 'emotional intelligence' in young children in enabling them to feel capable and positive people.[2] Emotional intelligence is the ability to identify, use, understand and manage one's emotions in positive and constructive ways. It is about recognizing your own emotional state and the emotional states of others. Emotional intelligence is also about engaging with others in ways that draw people to you. Children with emotional intelligence are thought to pay attention and remember better (links here with cognition).

Getting stressed emotionally happens to us all, including children. If one child wants a particular toy and someone else has it, the inclination to grab it off the other child is strong. Children who have learned to control their emotions and impulses realize that turn-taking, sharing and resolving such conflicts can be achieved in other ways. It is up to practitioners to give gentle guidance and consistent support – as well as to listen – to children who are experiencing such feelings and help them to convert negative emotions into positive ones. When the child who has taken the toy can empathize with the distressed child and hand over the toy with a smile and a touch, this child has well-developed emotional intelligence. Emotional tantrums are a way for very young children to express themselves because they may not yet have the words. The development of speech allows more emotional control.

When a child says 'Gita won't play with me' that child is exhibiting emotional stress: it might seem like something very insignificant to the practitioner but it represents deep-seated hurt to the child and should be handled sensitively by talking to young children about their emotions, both positive and negative. Resolving conflicts in healthy and constructive ways will then enable children to develop trust between themselves and other children and adults in their play interactions and relationships. After all, all of us have common emotions such as sadness, fear, anger and happiness.

Practitioners need to model effective emotional behaviours in the way they interact with children; for example, showing emotional control when children's play appears to be too noisy or exuberant, recognizing that their own emotional (re)actions and the physical environment may all influence. When emotions run high it is often possible to use humour (another aspect of play) to change the ethos to one of playful co-operation. Contexts that emphasize social competences also stimulate effective learning[3] and imaginative play, thought to diminish aggression and promote emotional intelligence.[4]

There are long-term effects noted in relation to good emotional 'health' that 'helps protect children against emotional and behavioural problems, violence and crime, teenage pregnancy and the misuse of drugs and alcohol,'[5] – a big claim!

Environments for play

It is vital that those in early childhood settings create environments that invite exploration and play both indoors and outdoors. This section concentrates on the indoor environment that should, first and foremost, be welcoming to children and parents. The environment they enter should look as though it is interesting, playful and organized with children's interests and learning in mind. Part of organizing the environment, once one understands the children's interests and motivations, is to make it welcoming for *every* child. This means ensuring that there is, for example, accessibility for those with individual needs to access the play opportunities and materials. It also means ensuring that family and community backgrounds are considered and practitioners have ensured that the classroom is welcoming to those with different cultural and ethnic origins.

In *Reggio Emilia* preschools, the context for learning was perceived by Malaguzzi as 'part of the individual so that any response to a request we make to the children or request that the children make of adults is facilitated or obstructed by the environment and its characteristics.'[6] One English study of young children found that attending settings (schools) with limited space and inappropriate play resources tended to perform less well academically than children attending schools with better facilities.[7]

It is vital the play resources and materials are located in such a way that children can make informed decisions and choices.[8] A common practice is to put playthings and materials out on tables but this needs careful thought. Practitioners should ask themselves whether this is, in fact, promoting self-regulation and choice or whether it would be better to have clearly labelled equipment that children can select for themselves and then use in an area of the setting they select. Ensuring children know where everything is (and ensuring that they relocate it when their activity is complete) presents a far more effective environment for developing children's confidence, self-efficacy and security and allows the play and learning that emerges to be based on real child-initiated experiences. This arrangement might, as in the case of HighScope, include the area being split into themes; for example, sand/water play, language/literacy, home/role play, construction and so on. Occasionally arranging new items on tables or floor space to promote or extend children's

Photograph E1 Environment for small world play

interest in a particular topic can invite the children into a different play focus and ignite or excite new interests. This is particularly useful when some children have taken particular interest in, for example, how they get to school and a map might be constructed with model houses, roadways and little people.

The play materials included in the environment need to be flexible and open-ended so that children can move their chosen resources to different parts of the room (or even outdoors) and engage in different types of play. It also needs to provide opportunities for different forms of interaction between adults and children and between children themselves. Effective learning environments need to relate to real life as children like to feel they are part of the real world: this means using (at least some of the time) actual items, especially in providing things like woodwork tools the balance of which is 'correct' in adult (but small) tools but unbalanced in children's tools. Children cannot get a sense of weight/heaviness, texture, careful handling and so on with toy plastic tools! The same applies to plastic fruit and vegetables.

Example E1

The shop area has real fruit and vegetables that the reception year children are arranging into baskets they have selected for the purpose from a range available. They have recently visited the local greengrocer and are discussing in detail how the goods should be arranged. Archie and Lucy have a disagreement about which is the best way not to squash the grapes that Sophie solves by fetching some pieces of clean sponge. Real money exchanges hands when shop-play begins. The following day, the children are involved in making fruit salad for snack time with vegetable soup following the next day!

The play environment needs to offer quality in many ways; for example, time, peace and quiet, noise, places to talk and make marks, challenge and mental stimulation, motivation to learn, the use of all children's senses, the opportunity to play alone or with others, movement experiences, natural world opportunities, costumes to experience being like other people and a chance to express feelings.[9]

Exploratory/epistemic play

Children engaged through their play in exploring the world learn to develop a perception of themselves as competent, self-assured learners who know that it is all right to ask questions, make mistakes and discover things for yourself. Is play and exploration, then, one and the same? The most extensive research in this area was conducted in the 1970s by Corinne Hutt, who concluded that exploration and play were somewhat different. She saw exploration as the handling of materials and the raising of the question 'What does this thing do?,' whereas in play children are more concerned with what they can do with an object. It was Hutt who used the term 'epistemic behaviour' for exploration (and 'ludic' for play behaviours), '. . . fuelled by their inquisitiveness as they search for understanding.'[10] While gathering information about the object, acquiring skills including problem solving and understanding of the characteristics of that object are inherent in epistemic play, ludic play is more to do with enjoyment, fun and imagination.

My work used Hutt's basic classification for observing children's play but my observations suggested that divisions between exploratory play and ludic play were inconsistent. As children learn through all their senses, so they play through all their senses and the sensory information-gathering (exploration) is as much part of the play as the later, more imaginative or creative, elements – just a different form of play. And to me there is also another stage when children come upon something unexpected and need to problem-solve. My proposal is that playful exploration is a forerunner to more pure play and that ultimately children through both processes come upon 'challenges.'[11] As an example (and I have used similar examples with adults with similar findings), when a child is presented with a new material, say clay or dough, they will first press, push, punch, squeeze, stretch and so on (exploratory/epistemic play) and in so doing learn about properties. They then often want to make something with the dough, perhaps a figure (ludic play) but find that it will not stand on two legs because of the soft properties of the dough. The model may either then be destroyed or started again or the legs might be pulled off and different ones made or the person might be made to sit down (a problem discovered and solved). In this latter instance, they are also learning that different materials have different 'rules' (the third stage of Hutt's model is games with rules but, in this example, it is not really a game but rather the clay that is 'ruled-based'). This process shows the integration of pure play, playful learning and playful teaching.[12] Studies have shown that, through exploration, children appear to readily learn causal relationships that leads them later more systematically into scientific enquiry.[13]

Another link with research is that which has examined exploration of materials and used comparisons between a control group of young children who have had the chance for exploratory play and a group who are given a task without prior experience. In each case, those children who have engaged in exploratory play do better on a subsequent devised task; for example, in 3–5-year-olds' explorations, construction and tool use during play positively correlated to performance in later tasks.[14]

We must also remember that children of whatever age, and particularly babies and toddlers, do not make any distinction between these forms of play: all they are concerned about is whether something attracts their attention and can be explored.

References

1. Bruce, T. (2004) *Developing Learning in Early Childhood*. London: Paul Chapman.
2. Goleman, D. (2005) *Emotional Intelligence: Why It Can Matter More than IQ* (2nd edn.) New York: Random House.
3. Morais, A. and Rocha, C. (1999) Development of social competences in the primary school – study of specific pedagogic practices, *British Educational Research Journal*, 26(1): 92–119.
4. Holland, P. (2003) *We Don't Play With Guns Here: Weapons and Superhero Play in the Early Years*. Maidenhead: Open University Press.
5. Adi, Y., Killoran, A., Janmohamed, K. et al. (2007) *Systematic Review of the Effectiveness of Interventions to Promote Mental Wellbeing in Children in Primary Education. Report 1*. London: National Institute for Health and Clinical Excellence.
6. Gandini, L. (1998) Educational and caring spaces. In C. Edwards, L. Gandini and G. Forman (eds) *The Hundred Languages of Children: The Reggio Emilia Approach – Advance Reflections*. Greenwich, CN: Ablex Publishing.
7. Smith, P.K. and Connolly, K.J. (1980) *The Ecology of Preschool Behaviour*. Cambridge: Cambridge University Press. (Note: There appears to be little current or more recent research on indoor play environments and their effects on children's learning.)
8. Trudell, P. (2010) A place for play: creating complex learning environments. In J. Moyles (ed.) *Thinking about Play: Developing a Reflective Approach*. Maidenhead: Open University Press.
9. Play Wales (2009) *When We Value Children's Play, We Value Children*. Cardiff. Available online at www.playwales.org.uk/page.asp?id=52 (accessed 15 January 2012).
10. Hutt, S., Tyler, S., Hutt, C. and Christopherson, H. (1989) *Play, Exploration and Learning*. London: Routledge.
11. Moyles, J. (1989) *Just Playing? The Role and Status of Play in Early Education*. Maidenhead: Open University Press.
12. Moyles, J. (2010) Practitioner reflection on play and playful pedagogies. In J. Moyles (ed.) *Thinking about Play: Developing a Reflective Approach*. Maidenhead: Open University Press.

13. Cook, C., Goodman, N. and Schulz, L. (2011) Where science starts: spontaneous experiments in preschoolers' exploratory play, *Cognition*, 120(3): 341–49.
14. Hirsh-Pasek, K., Golinkoff, R., Berk, L. and Singer D. (2008) *A Mandate for Playful Learning in Preschool: Presenting the Evidence*. New York: Oxford University Press.

F

First-hand experience (see also exploratory/epistemic play)

First-hand experience is active playful engagement with things and playing with ideas, both of which promote mental activity which helps young children to retain new learning and integrate it with what they already know: this is the basis of first-hand experience. Being told something is just not the same as finding out for oneself! Admittedly, gathering your own information in this way can be long-winded and frustrating and we cannot all experience everything in order to understand – sometimes there is a case for telling, modelling or using some other means to support a child's understanding. But anything outside the realm of children's first-hand, play experiences is difficult for them to understand in the early years and, therefore, experiences presented to children should (1) have a basis in something they can do for themselves, and (2) be playful.

Sadly this is not always the case: research has shown that there is an urgent need to reinstate play and first-hand experience as core elements of children's learning experiences in reception classes, which are often dominated by worksheets or whole-class, didactic teaching.[1] Experiential learning is often messy and can, therefore, be avoided by those who are concerned that children look as though they are 'working' properly. But

> The child is curious. He [sic] wants to make sense out of things, find out how things work, gain competence and control over himself and his environment. He is open, perceptive, and experimental ... he does not merely observe the world around him ... but tastes it,

touches it, hefts it, bends it, breaks it. To find out how reality works, he works on it … He is not afraid of making mistakes. And he is patient. He can tolerate an extraordinary amount of uncertainty, confusion, ignorance, and suspense. … School is not a place that gives much time, or opportunity, or reward, for this kind of thinking and learning.[2]

Experiential play and learning has the power of the new! Doing things for the first time teaches us new things and encourages us to use language to make sense of the experience and tell others about it. Experiential, hands-on opportunities also enable children to practise, master and consolidate previous learning and make them feel confident and motivated to learn skills, as well as develop an understanding of themselves and their world. First-hand experience of different social situations enables children to learn about relationships, feelings, disappointments, joys – even shame and guilt – absorbed in a safe and secure environment with caring adults.

Photograph F1 Learning from first-hand experience

Theorists strongly believe that by playfully

handling objects and observing things in their world, children begin to compare them. They classify and sequence objects and things, relating new information to their existing ideas of how the world works ... When information doesn't fit their existing ideas, they change these or create new ones ... Through daily, first-hand experiences, children have the opportunity to confirm or change their ideas about how things work and what they can do with the things in their world. These initial, often incomplete and tentative, hypotheses and schemes about their world are the foundation on which all subsequent learning is built.[3]

Flow/free-flow play

Flow/free-flow play indicates play without any impediment that enhances a child's or adult's feeling of happiness. It is a state of fluidity and represents the integration of play, love and work, as with Olympic athletes, who play at their work and work at their play and love what they do![4] Flow represents optimal levels of challenge; a sense of complete control; attention focused so strongly on the activity that feelings of self-consciousness and awareness of time disappear.

Play is so fluid that it cannot be defined purely as one aspect or another – it changes its nature and style to fit its environment, circumstances and the players involved, taking on different forms, expressions and meanings to the players concerned: that is the basis of free-flow play. It has intrinsic meaning to the children and may change direction at any moment, according to the children's needs and personalities, making it extremely difficult to 'use' as a tool for teaching. 'The whole point about play is that it cannot be pinned down. It flows. It is on the move.'[5] It can continue where it was left or can be restarted and flow in an entirely different direction if obstacles do not restrict the play.

Settings that offer free-flow play, where children are able to move independently and freely in their environment, appear to allow for more physically active play among the children.[6] The combination of busy lifestyles and academic commitments has impinged on children's free time and, therefore, their free-flow play and has, as a result, affected their cognitive, physical, social and emotional stability. 'Play that is directed by adults seems not to require the same level of skill, initiative and decision-making and so does not offer the same learning experience.'[7] Free-flow play has the potential to improve many aspects of emotional well-being such as minimizing anxiety, depression, aggression and sleep problems.[8]

Csikszentmihalyi identifies the factors shown in Table F1 as accompanying an experience of flow: most, but not all, are needed for flow to be experienced.

Table F1 The state of flow according to Mihaly Csikszentmihalyi[9] (adapted)

Involvement	Clear goals, complete focus and concentration, due to innate curiosity or training
Delight	A sense of joy and positive detachment from reality, lack of self-consciousness
Clarity	Greater inner clarity and built-in understanding of current needs
Challenge	Challenge that is neither too easy nor too hard, direct and immediate feedback
Confidence	Innate sense that the activity is achievable and that the individual's skills are adequate. No feelings of anxiety or boredom
Serenity	A sense of peace and an absence of worries about self
Timeliness	A focus on the present and a lack of attention to the passing of time
Motivation	Intrinsic understanding about what is needed and a desire to keep the momentum of the play going

The state of flow – what children (and adults) experience

In relation to children's play, free-flowing play is said to be an 'integrating mechanism' by which a child brings together various aspects of prior learning experience and in doing this arrives at new understanding.[10] Play is thought to come from within the child and does not progress through a sequence or hierarchy. Children wallow in ideas, feelings and relationships and become technically proficient.[11] Free-flow play has significant intensity (see Example F1) and needs practitioners to develop very flexible timetabling and to learn how to interact with children without interference!

Example F1

Hanya, aged 3, is out walking in the park with her big brother. She sees a large pile of leaves and runs towards them, jumping in them and then throwing them around. She flings herself down on them and spreads them, making 'angel wings' in the leaves. She is totally absorbed in her own play. Later, she takes a pocketful of leaves home and lays them on her bedside table. She smells and feels them and talks to her brother about what she did in the park.

Forest School and play

Forest School and play is an outdoor learning context in which children visit forests and woodlands and learn personal, social and 'useful' skills through exploration and play. Forest School has been defined as 'an inspirational process that offers children ... opportunities to achieve and develop confidence through hands-on learning in a woodland environment.'[12] Forest School builds independence and self-esteem in school-age children: the play is frequently led by the children and their interests and provides regular opportunities to achieve and develop confidence and self-esteem through hands-on learning experiences in a local woodland environment. Such initiatives are also related to enabling children and adults to understand the forest as a sustainable environment.

Photograph F2 Out in the forest

As well as children becoming fitter and healthier by being in the outdoor environment, much research is showing the benefits not only of Forest School itself but of the need for children to be physically active if they are to concentrate and persevere in academic experiences.[13] Research has shown that play, in natural environments like Forest School, is more diverse, imaginative and creative[14] and improves children's cognitive development through greater awareness, reasoning and observation skills.[15] Given that, nowadays, playing outside can be very limited for young children as fears of safety, risk and liability influence parents and practitioners alike, Forest School provides an important opportunity for children to play, learn and socialize outdoors as well as combat a perceived 'nature deficit disorder'[16] (potentially created by the new technologies).

Massey sees the benefits of Forest School as a programme that evolves from the needs of the child and their interests, offering opportunities to build self-esteem through play and small achievable steps. It provides a context for real, meaningful language and communication and offers the practitioner alternative views of the child and different insights into a particular child's development. Forest School is beneficial to the child's all-round development, particularly in relation to social and emotional, allowing the children to take risks, problem-solve and use higher level thinking skills.[17] Perhaps as importantly, Forest School gives children freedom and independence not otherwise available to them, through making them aware of potential hazards and giving them the responsibility to take risks yet play safely.

Sara Knight, a UK expert in Forest School, says:

> For children in the early years Forest School means child-initiated activities supported by a trained Forest School practitioner that take place over time, typically once a week for at least ten weeks. Children are able to become involved in age-appropriate risky activities that engage them holistically with their environment and facilitate learning about that environment, about themselves and about how to get on with each other.[18]

Fun

Fun is often given a 'bad press;' for example, if it is fun children (and adults) cannot be 'working,' learning or being serious! But one could argue that if it is not fun then neither children nor adults will develop effective motivations and dispositions to 'work' and the business of learning. Fun is about enjoying life and feeling fulfilled, having a sense of humour and finding everyday activities pleasurable. The characteristics of fun are said to be that 'it is relative, situational, voluntary and natural. Fun can have a positive effect on the learning process by inviting intrinsic motivation, suspending social inhibitions, reducing stress and creating a state of relaxed alertness.'[19] Hear, hear!

References

1. Moyles, J. and Worthington, M. (2011) *The Early Years Foundation Stage Through the Daily Experiences of Children*. Occasional Paper No. 1, TACTYC: Association for the Professional Development of Early Years Educators. Available online at www.tactyc.org.uk. See also: Adams, S., Alexander, E., Drummond,

M.J. and Moyles, J. (2004) *Inside the Foundation Stage: Recreating the Reception Year*. London: Association of Teachers and Lecturers.

2. Holt, J. (1995) *How Children Learn*. New York: Perseus Books Group (p. 287). See also Holt, J. (2003) *Teach Your Own*. New York: Perseus Books Group (p. 128).

3. Seefeldt, C. and Galper, A. (2006) *Experience and Education: First-hand Experience*. Available online at www.education.com/reference/article/experience-education-firsthand (accessed 16 January 2012).

4. Elkind, D. (2007) *The Power of Play*. Philadelphia, PA: Da Capo Press (p. 13).

5. Bruce, T. (2004) *Developing Learning in Early Childhood 0–8*. London: Sage Publications (p. 154).

6. Brady, L.M., Gibb, J., Henshall, A. and Lewis, J. (2008) *Play and Exercise in Early Years: Physically Active Play in Early Childhood Provision*. Available online at www.culture.gov.uk/images/research/Playresearch2008 (accessed 15 June 2009).

7. Gleave, R. (2009) *Children's Time to Play: A Literature Review*. London: Play-day/Play England/NCB (p. 29). Available online at www.playday.org.uk/pdf/Childrens-time-to-play-a-literature-review.pdf (accessed 15 January 2012).

8. Burdette, H. and Whitaker, R. (2005) Resurrecting free play in young children looking beyond fitness and fatness to attention, affiliation, and effect, *Archives of Pediatrics and Adolescent Medicine*, 159(1): 46–50.

9. Csikszentmihalyi, M. (2002) *Flow: The Classic Work on How to Achieve Happiness* (2nd edn.) London: Random House (pp. 89–92).

10. Bruce, T. (1991) *Time to Play in Early Childhood Education*. London: Hodder & Stoughton.

11. Bruce, T. (ibid.)

12. O'Brien, L. and Murray, R. (2008) *Forest School Research Summary*. Forest Research: SERC. Available online at www.forestry.gov.uk/website/pdf.nsf/pdf/SERG_Forest_School_research_summary.pdf/FILE/SERG_Forest_School_research_summary.pdf (accessed 13 January 2012). See also O'Brien, L. and Murray, R. (2007) Forest School and its impacts on young children: case studies in Britain, *Urban Forestry and Urban Greening*, 6(4): 249–65.

13. Pellegrini, A. (1995) *School Recess and Playground Behaviour*. Albany, NY: State University of New York Press.

14. Fjortoft, I. (2001) The natural environment as a playground for children: the impact of outdoor play activities in pre-primary school children, *Early Childhood Education Journal*, 29(2): 111–17.

15. Pyle, Robert (2002). Eden in a vacant lot: special places, species and kids in community of life. In P.H. Kahn and S.R. Kellert (eds) *Children and Nature: Psychological, Sociocultural and Evolutionary Investigations*. Cambridge: MIT Press.

16. Louv, R. (2005) *Last Child in the Woods: Saving Our Children from Nature-deficit Disorder*. Chapel Hill, NC: Algonquin.

17. Massey, S. (undated) *The Benefits of a Forest School Experience for Children in their Early Years* (p. 8). Available online at www.worcestershire.gov. uk/cms/pdf/Worcs%20Forest%20School%20Research%20Academic%20 Journal.pdf (accessed 15 January 2012).
18. For more information see: Knight, S. (2013) *Forest School and Outdoor Learning in the Early Years* (2nd edn.). London: Publications Sage.
19. Bisson, C. and Luckner, J. (1996) Fun in Learning: the pedagogical role of fun in adventure education, *Journal of Experiential Education*, 19(2): 108–12.

G

Games play

Play and games includes sports, but for the purpose of this book I will restrict definitions to those associated with 'games with rules' specifically for younger children. Although young children can, for example, play football, they do it more for the fun of running about and being with others than for their understanding of the rules of the game – easily broken by young children anyway! Young children's games play will not usually have extrinsically imposed rules (as do sports) because until children reach understanding of 'fairness' (about age 6–7) the concept will elude them. Fairness means playing by the rules, taking turns, sharing and listening, notoriously difficult concepts the younger the player. This does not mean that we should not play games with children, because they help children develop their sense of justice, morals and ethics. Sadly, there appears to be a lack of 'traditional' games passed down from older to younger children in contemporary society, perhaps because of the individualized games on iPods and other technologies.

'It's not fair!' Learning rules and fairness through games ensures these difficult concepts have more meaning to children although young children have no predisposition to learning 'rules,' whatever those rules may be, whether numbers, letters or games rules. They need to attain 'reason,' which for most children is about 6–7-years-old. Simple rules can, however, give structure to play: for example, when children are developing a role-play context, or sharing the large outdoor toys. Rules such as Gussin-Paley's 'You can't say you can't play' led to children recognizing that it is not good to be or feel excluded by others.[1] 'Children as young as seven are just as likely as adults to do the right thing by their friends, in contrast to kids between three and four, who are almost universally selfish.'[2]

Game playing teaches children about taking turns, planning strategy, negotiation, social interaction, sequencing, rules, how to win and lose gracefully and co-operation. Simple board and card games like Ludo and Pelmanism (matching two hidden pictures) and making up your own games with your own rules are also vital features of young children's play and learning. So-called 'learning games' are often developed by practitioners to support children's learning through play, including games like 'letter bingo' and word/picture matching: these help to ensure that teaching is at least playful and being playful makes the activity more likely to get a positive response from children. A game such as doing a jigsaw puzzle has rules although it is more difficult for young children than most people realize. Because most young children perceive in wholes rather than in parts, jigsaws – except the inset board kind – are quite difficult and often need a lot of adult or older child support.

Photograph G1 Learning the rules of how to get along

Games in general support children's learning of 'rules' in a variety of ways: there are rules associated with music (you have to play the right notes to create a tune) and mathematics (you have to know that number elements are fixed, i.e. three is always three and zero is important in place value).[3] Role play often leads to games related to real or fantasy life where children themselves make the rules and determine what they and others can do.

Games involve co-operation and, for young children, just a hint of competition but this, on the whole, should be underplayed as there is plenty of time to learn the competitive spirit later. In the early years, children need to learn to care for each other, share generally and get along socially. Young children's games are generally for fun not for winning, so any 'clubs' (and there are burgeoning numbers even for very young children) should emphasize the active, healthy nature of the exercise rather than competition.

Gender and play

Gender is socially determined while sex is biological. Children are usually born boys or girls and the way they and others react to that designation, plus the body's own mechanisms and chemicals, result in behaviours that are then noted as 'gender-specific.' Children are socialized into gender-specific behaviours by their families, communities and early years settings, as well as the media. Parents often expect that girls will like dolls and home-related toys, whereas boys will like footballs and construction materials:[4] such attitudes will clearly impact upon children's self-knowledge. Toy shops, too, often promote such stereotyped attitudes clearly labelling some (pink and fluffy!) areas 'girls toys' and some (colourful and bold) sections 'boys toys.' Weekend television commercials regularly show girls playing with dolls or make-up and boys playing sports, racing cars or battling action figures: a powerful message for young children to absorb about play choices. 'Most children tend to accept sex stereotypes, identify with the stereotypical role of their gender, and punish other children, especially boys, who exhibit cross-gender behaviors and traits.'[5]

An investigation into 'how preschool children use gender-based reasoning in making judgements about toy preferences for themselves and others' showed preschool children unfamiliar, non-sex-typed toys and asked them to rate how much they, other girls, and other boys would like each toy, as expected, children made gender-based inferences. 'What I like, children of my sex will also like, and children of the other sex will not like.' Even with very attractive toys, children liked toys less if they were labelled as being for the other sex, and expected other girls and boys to do the same.[6]

Such gendered choices of toys and activities in play can be altered with adult intervention: for example, in one study, girls became more interested and involved in constructional play when they were given motivating tasks using these materials.[7] Boys, similarly, if offered 'boys only' time in the home area (often a girls' domain), more readily generate role play there. Yet all of us know that, given the chance, boys will turn anything into a weapon! This seems to be instinctual. A friend has two boys (aged 5 and 8, respectively) and a one-year-old girl, who has always played with her brothers' toys, but she has suddenly become doll aware and uses anything and everything wrapped up in various 'blankets' to be her 'doll.' Boys, in particular, play with toys that are consistent with their own gender. However, in research male-stereotyped toys resulted in simpler forms of play than female-stereotyped, which led to higher cognitive skills.[8]

Photograph G2 Same-sex role play

Even quite young children migrate to playing with same-sex children: 'Children's partner preferences were highly sex differentiated and stable over time . . . [and] the more both girls and boys played with same-sex partners, the more their behavior became sex differentiated.'[9] As Kelso (aged 5) suggests: 'The rule in the den is – NO GIRLS ALLOWED, no stealing and don't hit people with sticks – we obey it – well, ish!'[10]

References

1. Gussin-Paley, V. (1993) *You Can't Say You Can't Play*. Cambridge, MA: Harvard University Press.

2. Bernhard, H., Fischbacher, U. and Fehr, E. (2006) Parochial altruism in humans, *Nature*, 442 (7105): 912–15.

3. Griffiths, R. (2010) Mathematics and play. In J. Moyles (ed.) *The Excellence of Play* (3rd edn.). Maidenhead: Open University Press.

4. Yelland, N. (2005) *Critical Issues in Early Childhood Education*. Maidenhead: Open University Press. See also Browne, N. (2004) *Gender Equity in the Early Years*. Maidenhead: Open University Press.

5. Larson, M.S. (2001) Interactions, activities and gender in children's television commercials: a content analysis, *Journal of Broadcasting and Electronic Media*, 45(1): 41–57.

6. Martin, C., Eisenbud, L. and Rose, H. (1995) Children's gender-based reasoning about toys, *Child Development*, 66: 1453–71.

7. MacNaughton, G. (1997) Who's got the power? Rethinking gender equity strategies in early childhood, *International Journal of Early Years Education*, 5(1): 57–66.

8. Cheyney, I., Kelly-Vance, L., Gill-Glover, K., Ruane, A. and Ryalls, B. (2003) The effects of stereotyped toys on play assessment in children aged 18–47 months, *Educational Psychology*, 22(5): 95–106.

9. Martin, C. and Fabes, R. (2001) The stability and consequences of young children's same-sex peer interactions, *Developmental Psychology*, 37(3): 431–46.

10. Burns, V. and Irvine, C. (2011) *'I'd Play All Day and All Night If I Could ...' A Report on Children's Views of Their Right to Play*. Scotland: International Play Association. Available online at www.sol.co.uk/i/ipascotland/Right%20to%20play.pdf (accessed 17 January 2012) (p. 4).

H

Happiness (see E = Emotional development and play)
Health and play
Heuristic play
Holistic development and play (throughout the book)
Humour and play

Health and play

Whether parents or practitioners, we all want to do our best to ensure children in our care are healthy and happy players. Health means physical, mental and emotional health: lack of these impedes children's play and holistic development. A sickly child may not have the energy to play with others; an obese child may feel awkward and be rejected by other children. We know that playing has an impact on the physical and chemical development of the brain – it 'influences children's ability to adapt to, survive, thrive and shape their social and physical environments . . . Play can help build resilience – the capacity for children to thrive despite adversity and stress in their lives.'[1] It is vital that children have bumps and scrapes to teach them about what is and is not safe: children who grow up without experiencing any level of 'danger' are ill-equipped to deal with life's challenges.

We have seen (C = Consumerism) that modern electronic toys and playthings often limit children's physical activity as they are generally sedentary, individual games (with odd exceptions such as Wii Fit©, which encourages movement and exercise). Over-protection from parents can mean that children's opportunities to play outside with their friends – or even walk to school – are curtailed for the current generation of children.

Outdoor play and Forest School are just two examples of situations that are known to benefit children's health. Much research has shown that even short breaks enable children to regain equilibrium and concentration in learning experiences and currently there is much debate about the benefits of exercise for children's overall health. 'Outdoor exercise and play are most important as they have the biggest effect on health, especially in relation to

Photograph H1 The importance of physical play activity

their mental health and happiness.'[2] With increasing numbers of children suffering from overweight and obesity (now triple the numbers in 1970) as well as high blood pressure and cholesterol levels, there is a need to reassert the belief that, to sustain optimal health, all children require sustained physical activity every day.[3] Research suggests that children can gain more physical exercise in regular informal play than in a weekly sports activity, and walking and playing provide children with more physical activity than most other events in their lives.[4]

While exercising through play is the most obvious health issue, nutrition can also be worrying with young children; that is, when they refuse to eat or have poor nutrition due to poverty or lack of parental knowledge. Adequate nutrition is known to be important in accident prevention because, for example, the child who arrives at school having eaten little or no breakfast may experience low blood sugar levels and be 'clumsy' – slowed reaction times and being less alert can cause children to be more accident-prone.[5]

Making mealtimes more playful than stressful can mean that 'fussy eaters' are encouraged to try different foods. Turning sausage, mash and peas into a funny face on the plate, as many parents will know, can mean the difference between a child eating or not! Playing 'aeroplanes' with the spoon for the baby can make a mealtime far more enjoyable and successful! In addition, the majority of young children are fascinated by cooking, and helping them to be involved playfully in preparing and presenting foods for others can be a delightful way of enabling them to acquire a basic understanding of different food values and good eating habits.

Other issues in relation to health and play are fun bedtimes so that regular sleep patterns are established; washing hands, which often needs to be playfully experienced and fun if it is to be repeated regularly; and lathering protective sun cream on tender skins before outdoor play.

Heuristic play

Closely linked with trial and error learning and exploratory/epistemic play, heuristic play opportunities are an experience-based intuitive means for problem solving, learning and discovery. Heuristic play is founded in children's natural curiosity and their drive to manipulate through all their senses. Very young children are fascinated to explore what things are and what things do: heuristic play allows them to use sensory experiences to make such discoveries. In heuristic, experimental, free-flow play, children begin to categorize objects, which precedes the development of more complex knowledge and understanding in mathematics and science.[6]

'Heuristic' derives from a Greek word *heuriskein* (to discover) and is related to 'eureka' (celebrate a discovery). Our current interpretation of heuristic play began with the seminal work of Goldschmied and Jackson:[7] they built on the notion of 'treasure baskets' – a collection of open-ended, safe, everyday objects, mainly from the natural and real world; for example, fir cones, wooden spoons, woolly pompoms, brushes, ribbons, chains and whole dried oranges. Nowadays practitioners tend to use any suitable receptacles (e.g. cardboard boxes or fabric bags), the emphasis being on natural materials rather than on plastics that tend to all feel the same irrespective of what the object is.

The aim of treasure baskets and heuristic play is to 'encourage complex, concentrated play in preference to aimless flitting from one thing to another.'[8] It is emphasized that 'Heuristic play is an approach and not a prescription. There is no right way to do it and people in different settings will have their own ideas and collect their own materials':[9] ideas for practitioners are abundant ([10,11]). The role of the adult is to act as an 'emotional anchor' and foster confidence and concentration while remaining a non-participant observer.

As well as developing an understanding of concepts such as movement, shape, space, mass, length, weight, one-to-one correspondence and seriation as they select items, the benefits of heuristic play to young children aged between a few months and about 3 are thought to be the:

- stimulus to make choices and decisions and show preferences;
- expression of pleasure and fun;
- increase in concentration;

- interest and stimulation of all the senses provided by the variety and textures of objects;
- open-endedness and real world, meaningful nature of the playthings;
- opportunity for continual practice and mastery leading to self-confidence;
- endless possibilities for exploration, concentration and causal learning;
- manipulability of the articles and their affordability;
- development of fine motor skills and hand–eye co-ordination;
- creation of vital connections in the brain;
- building of confidence and self-esteem;
- encouragement of problem solving and creativity;
- increased support for the development of speech and language.[12]

Children over 3-years-old have been found to use treasure baskets for stimulating role play and language and literacy play, and they are also known to be invaluable for children with individual and special needs requiring sensory experiences. The use of treasure baskets links closely with the development of schema.

Humour and play

> Why did the clock get sick?..................... It was run down!
> Why was the broom late?....................... It over swept!

These typical children's jokes give an insight into other aspects of their play – humour, laughter and, in this case, play on words. Children are thought to laugh about 200 times a day whereas an adult might manage 20. Children will often laugh at these plays on words even if they do not exactly 'get it' but they understand the context of a 'joke.' Children's verbal humour depends a lot on parody;[13] that is, changing words in order to make the song 'funny' – for example, 'Happy Birthday to you, squashed tomatoes and stew...' and so on – as well as changes to playground chants and rhymes. Playful tricks are also part of children's humour from a young age, like hiding a toy and telling the adult it is lost!

The root of all humour is play in adults and children – it is play with, for example, ideas, memories and comic situations. Like adults, children find humour in incongruity; that is, when our logical expectations do not match up with the end of the situation or the joke. So if a child expects you to pull a teddy from behind your back and it is a shoe, that is incongruous. We laugh for relief when tension is built up and we need a release of emotion,

Photograph H2 Daddy, you're making me laugh!

and this might be related to a humorous character, scene or funny dialogue or just something that brings an amusing incident to mind. In children who are worried about their reading, a puppet popping up to say that it finds reading difficult can make them laugh and ease the situation. So-called 'slapstick' comedy is when we laugh at someone else's mistakes: this kind of humour is very much a 'childlike' humour and is typified by people falling over in a comic way. Research has shown that '... during humorous events children are involved in play activity such as: (1) play with materials; (2) play with language; (3) pretend play; (4) physical play.' This researcher also found that children turned routines into playful humorous events and concluded that children were engaged in 'socio-cognitive attributes, such as social interaction, creative thinking and metacognitive experience' during humorous play episodes.[14]

Humour, like play, has health benefits in that laughter releases both endorphins in the brain that are connected with the 'feel-good effect'[15] and also a natural tranquilizer that can relieve pain. It is thought that play and laughter relaxes the whole body, boosts the immune system and protects the heart by increasing the blood flow. Play and laughter readies you to join in the fun – it is contagious! For all these reasons and more, it is important for adults to share humour with children but ensure that they are laughing *with* children rather than *at* them. Laughter is a 'signal of encouragement to continue' and,

Table H1 The development of humour in babies and children

Age	Humour response	Developmental issue	Adult interaction
Birth–4 mths	Smiling	Playful response to sights, sounds, movements, feeding	Provide environment
4–8 mths	Laughter at physical level with verbal/active playful stimulation	Discovering body movements, recognition of human faces and voices	Engage in physical playful contact
8 mths–1 yr	Laughs when in contact with playthings	Object constancy – distinguishing between self and 'other'	Peek-a-boo, contact play with toys
1–2 yrs	Incongruent behaviours	Developing organized schemas	Mislabelling, playing with toys in different or unexpected ways
2–4 yrs	Fantasy, make-believe, slapstick play, silly words and songs, bodily noises, direct, first-hand playful experiences	Mastery of motor skills, development of symbols, awareness of bodily functions, creation of novel stimulus	Play house, active play, simple songs and rhymes
5–10 yrs	Riddles and simple word incongruencies.	Ability to detect transitions and relationships in playful contexts	Joke books, cartoon, humour repeated over and over

for babies, 'it is a critical way of communicating with their mothers before they can speak, so their laughter encourages maternal attention.'[16] Children also use humour as a means of working out fears, anxieties and conflicts. The stages of children's humour development are outlined in Table H1.[17]

References

1. Lester, S. and Russell, W. (2008) *Play for a Change: Play Policy and Practice: A Review of Contemporary Perspectives.* London: Play England (p. 12).
2. Health Protection Agency (2009) *A Children's Environment and Health Strategy for the UK.* London: HPA (p. 23).

3. Waite-Stupiansky, S. and Findlay, M. (2001) The fourth R: recess and its link to learning, *Educational Forum*, 66(1): 16–24.

4. Mackett, R. (2004) *Making Children's Lives More Active*. University College London. Available online at www.eprints.ucl.ac.uk/1346/1/2004_39.pdf (accessed 18 January 2012).

5. Marotz, L. (2011) *Health, Safety and Nutrition for the Young Child* (8th edn.). Belmont, CA: Wadsworth.

6. Siraj-Blatchford, J. and Siraj-Blatchford, I. (2002) Developmentally appropriate technology in early childhood: 'video conferencing' – a limit case? *Journal of Contemporary Issues in Early Education*, 3(2): 216–25.

7. Goldschmied, E. and Jackson, S. (2005) *People Under Three: Young Children in Day Care* (2nd edn.). London: Routledge.

8. Goldschmied, E. and Jackson, S. (ibid.) (p. 9).

9. Goldschmied, E. and Jackson, S. (ibid.) (p. 130).

10. Hughes, A. (2006) *Developing Play for the Under-3s: Treasure Baskets and Heuristic Play*. Oxford: David Fulton.

11. Nutbrown, C. and Page, J. (2008) *Working with Babies and Children From Birth-to-Three*. London: Sage Publications (p. 155).

12. Based on Gascoyne, S. (2012) Seeing the wood for the trees: adults' roles in supporting sensory play. In T. Papatheodorou and J. Moyles (eds) *Cross-cultural Perspectives on Early Childhood*. London: Sage Publications.

13. *Children's Playground Games and Songs in the New Media Age* 2009–2011: Project Report. Universities of London, Sheffield and East London and the British Library Arts. London: Arts and Humanities Research Council.

14. Loizou, E. (2005) Humor: a different kind of play, *European Early Childhood Education Research Journal*, 13(2): 97–109.

15. Dunbar, R. (2011) Social laughter is correlated with an elevated pain threshold. Proceedings of the Royal Society Biological Sciences. Published online 14 September. Available at www.rspb.royalsocietypublishing.org/content/early/2011/09/19/rspb.2011.1373.full.pdf+html (accessed 16 January 2012).

16. Weisfeld, G.E. (2006) Humor appreciation as an adaptive esthetic emotion, *International Journal of Humor Research*, 19: 1–26.

17. Adapted from Puder, C. (1998) The healthful effects of laughter, *Journal of Child and Youth Care*, 12(3): 45–53.

I

Iconic and symbolic learning and play

Bruner[1] defined several, loosely sequential developmental stages that children go through in order to learn and understand concepts: enactive, iconic and symbolic play. Enactive play (action-based) is the first stage and could also be classed as the exploratory, discovery stage (heuristic). Iconic (image-based) play is when children begin to understand the icons or representations of objects even if they cannot actually touch or feel the objects. The symbolic stage (language-based) is when children are able to understand and make symbols and this is the most sophisticated and advanced stage. Put into a practical context, the child at the enactive level will enjoy playing with coins and handling real money; at the iconic stage, the child will understand that a picture of coins in a book represents those things that they have handled; at the symbolic stage, the child will be able to understand and manipulate symbols that represent coins; for example, £1 or 50p.

These stages even apply to adults when they are faced with new learning so it is easy to see why they are so important for young children. Moving them through the playful enactive and iconic stages too quickly will mean that they will struggle with symbolic understanding: again, a practical example would be where children are expected to understand how to manipulate numbers (symbols) without sufficient enactive play. Many adults, particularly policy

Table I1 Relating Bruner's stages to computers and electronic toys[2]

DOING	mouse	*enactive*	know where you are, manipulate
with IMAGES	icons, windows	*iconic*	recognize, compare, configure, make concrete
makes SYMBOLS	Smalltalk	*symbolic*	tie together long changes of reasoning, abstract

makers, tend to underestimate how much enactive and iconic play children need before they can cope with number and letter symbols.

More recently, iconic learning has been associated with new technologies and particularly computers and electronic games where children have to understand the icons in order to operate the games. Some believe that the real enactive play phase is missing in computer games but Kay has made a relationship between computers and Bruner's stages (see Table I1).

But one might still ask, where is the play? It would seem that children naturally move to playing with computers: '... children "possess a powerful form of media literacy," a spontaneous natural wisdom that is somehow denied to adults ... Far from destroying "natural" human relationships and forms of learning, digital technology ... liberate[s] children's innate spontaneity and imagination.'[3]

Imaginative play/imaginary friends

> Imagination is more important than knowledge. Knowledge is limited. Imagination encircles the world.
>
> (Albert Einstein 1879–1955)

Imagination and imaginative play enable the brain to represent images and icons, vital for children's learning eventually to read, write and understand mathematics: to think in the abstract. It also enables children to view the world from different perspectives and prepares them to handle change. It is important for early years practitioners not to underestimate the importance of imaginative play as 'It draws upon children's capacities for constructing meaning, framing stories, and making sense of their worlds in ways that enrich the development of the individual and the group simultaneously.'[4]

According to John Holt, children who are good at imagining and fantasizing are better at both learning about the world and coping with its surprises and disappointments. 'In fantasy we have a way of trying out situations, to get some feel of what they might be like, or how we might feel in them, without having to risk too much. It also gives us a way of coping with bad experiences, by letting us play and replay them in our mind until they have lost much of their power to hurt, or until we can make them come out in ways that leave us feeling less defeated and foolish.'[5] Advice to practitioners suggests '...children's imaginative play thrives on unpromising contexts, on hidden nooks and crannies, on secret codes and languages. Too much planning, provision ... may constrain rather than enable play.'[6]

So, too, with an 'Imaginary friend [who] can act as a surrogate for the child's wild-side.'[7] Imaginary friends are often created by young children: it is thought that 'by the age of seven, sixty-five percent of children ... have had an imaginary companion at some point in their lives.'[8] They are fictional characters (people, animals, robots) created as a playmate: they belong to that one child and to no one else and are a natural part of growing up. They may seem real to the child although their fictitious nature can also be recognized.[9] Children 'believe' in Father Christmas and the reality of some television characters, and some imaginary friends are based on such characters. In one study, children often interrupted conversations about their invisible companions to explain: 'It's not true, you know. It's only pretend.'[10]

Children often express their own feelings by attributing them to their imaginary companion who can then exhibit the full range of 'good' and 'bad' behaviours (See Example I1).

Example I1

Sam's imaginary friend is a rabbit named 'Solly.' They play together indoors and outside. When Sam is being good eating his dinner, he tells his mum 'Solly and I are eating our vegetables!' However, when Sam does not want to go to bed, he tells his mum 'Solly isn't tired: he wants me to play with him!'

Preschool children with make-believe friends engage in more imaginative play, have richer vocabularies and language skills and can entertain themselves more readily and get along better with classmates.[11] Whatever their purposes, having imaginary friends indicates a fertile, healthy and playful child.

Inclusion, equality and play

To be included in play is every child's right, irrespective of their individual or special needs, be they disability, language, culture, background, gender or behaviour. This has been recognized in play policies across various countries including the UK:[12] when we consider every child's right to play, this must concern the rights of *every* child. Some barriers to inclusion are physical – children cannot access the play spaces or areas – but some barriers are attitudinal, when we believe that children cannot be involved because they have a disability. Others are social and related to whether the disabled child and others believe that they can be socially integrated in play contexts alongside their peers. In early years settings all of these will need to be considered and handled sensitively and professionally: it is every child's right to access the same play and playful provision as every other child in that setting. 'Very often there is a focus on children's care needs rather than their need to play'[13] but 'enabling all children to play, and to play together, is about a benefit to the whole community.'[14]

When it comes to equality, treating children equally does not mean treating them all the same! For each child to be able to play in their own way their individual needs and dispositions have to be taken into account – children will have play preferences when it comes to other children but practitioners who note that some children are avoiding others because of skin colour or disability should observe closely the context of children's play and see if there is something evident that is causing some children to be rejected by others. Young children are not oblivious to racial differences; in fact, racism and stereotyping are known to occur before a child is 3[15] and it is up to practitioners to ensure that children learn early that stereotyping is neither helpful nor conducive to harmony in their play or lives. Children will learn tolerance only by seeing the attitudes exhibited by others towards people who are different in some way from themselves.

Experts Jane Lane and Haki Kapasi write:

> We know children learn by observing and absorbing messages from the world around them and reveal their observations in their play, for example evidence of family life in role plays. It is therefore logical that children will demonstrate society's attitudes towards differences and race in their play – attitudes that unwittingly reflect society's racism. Very young children do not have the capacity to filter out harmful messages about race, particularly when left unchallenged, and they learn to associate positive and negative attributes to people with different skin colours and facial features. Skilful practitioners will find observable evidence of this learning in children's play; for example, they will notice that children from minority ethnic communities play together when they are in a minority, but it does require huge honesty to admit the evidence and a commitment to take action to address it.[16]

Practitioners need playful, creative thinking in order to engage *all* children in play and playful learning contexts and to give them a range of choices and a sense of belonging and feeling welcome by focusing on their interests, skills, enthusiasms and personalities.[17] A rich play and playful environment will provide a range of sensory experiences for young children and ensure that all children have equal and varied opportunities to play with others as well as opportunities for achieving their individual play and learning potential.[18] It may be necessary to adapt the environment or the approach to give all children exhilarating play opportunities. When we speak to young children of varied abilities and capabilities, accessing the outdoor place spaces is high on their list of priorities.[19] Disabled children, in particular, often miss out on 'messy' play as parents often worry about 'appearances' but paint, mud, water, sand and clay are, arguably, even more important for such children to experience.

Practitioners should also be aware of the potential of play for the early identification of children with particular learning and development needs and be sensitive but firm with those who exhibit racist behaviour. Observation of children's play can give powerful and unique indicators of their learning styles, preferences, abilities, skills and understanding and opportunities for practitioners to remedy such indicators as relevant.

Independence and self-regulation in play

Children's independence, or autonomy, in play and learning contexts is now more usually referred to as 'self-regulation' so this will be the terminology used here. Self-regulation is the ability to control and direct one's own feelings, thoughts and actions. Self-regulated play is that which the child has freely chosen and which they want to pursue for themselves for its appeal to them emotionally, mentally and physically. Self-directed, independent play is thought in particular to nourish and support children's maturing mental abilities.[20] It is not about just being able to 'get on' independently in the classroom – in play or otherwise: it is about children understanding more about their own meta-cognition and taking responsibility for their own decisions in how they learn.

Self-regulation involves the capacity to do something one maybe does not want to do but because it is necessary, such as awaiting one's turn or raising one's hand.[21] Self-regulation in play requires practitioners to respect and value (and show that they value) children's choices – to say to a child deeply engrossed in play 'Leave that now and come and do some work with me' is not respectful however much the adult feels that the task they want to impose on the child is more important than what could be a deeply involved play episode! But self-regulation does not grow out of nothing: socially constructed learning requires support from others in the Vygotskian tradition. Children gradually acquire self-regulation through practitioners operating from a belief that children are competent players and learners and that what they need is not 'instruction' but learning strategies.

Photograph I1   Taking responsibility for one's own learning

Example I2

Vijay (aged 5) is playing with some paper making it into a boat shape. He has told the adult that he wants to 'make a boat that floats.' Several attempts later the boat structures are sodden and merely go 'squishy' in the water. The practitioner asks if he has any ideas about what the problem is. Vijay suggests that the paper is too 'thin' and, after further discussion and much feeling of textures, he chooses some waxed paper the practitioner has carefully included. He drips some water on it and is delighted that it rolls off without affecting the paper. His resultant boat floats beautifully.

Example I2 shows how a practitioner supported a child in developing his independence and self-regulation. He has used prior learning and made decisions seemingly from his own knowledge and was clearly intrinsically motivated in this boat play. He has planned and monitored changes to earlier ideas, persisted in the face of challenge[22] and learned that his earlier 'failure' providing a new learning opportunity with the support of the adult. Practitioners must make play and games a major part of their pedagogy: young children learn best through activities that they, not adults, instigate and regulate.[23]

David Whitebread, a psychologist and researcher with a particular expertise in self-regulation asserts:

> The importance of these self-regulatory abilities has been increasingly recognised in recent years, as research evidence has shown self-regulation to be the most powerful predictor of academic and many other aspects of development and well-being. Numerous intervention studies have also shown that even very young children can be taught to improve their self-regulatory abilities.[24]

References

1. See McLeod, S.A. (2008) *Simply Psychology: Bruner – Modes of Representation*. Available online at www.simplypsychology.org/bruner.html (accessed 16 January 2012).
2. Cited in www.learningspaces.org/n/papers/play2.html (accessed 3 February 2012).
3. Buckingham, D. (2000) *After the Death of Childhood: Growing Up in the Age of Electronic Media*. Cambridge: Polity Press (pp. 41, 44).
4. Kernan, M. (2007) *Play as a Context for Early Learning and Development: A Research Paper*. Dublin: National Council for Curriculum and Assessment (NCCA).
5. Holt, J. and Farenga, P. (2003) *Teach Your Own: The John Holt Book of Homeschooling*. Cambridge, MA: Perseus Publishers (p. 128).
6. Institute of Education (2011) *Children's Playground Games and Sons in the New Media Age: Project Report 2009–2011*. London: Centre for the Study of Children, Youth and Media (p. 11).
7. Elkind, D. (2007) *The Power of Play: Learning What Comes Naturally*. Philadelphia, PA: Da Capo Press (p. 115).
8. University of Washington (2004) *Two-thirds of School-age Children Have An Imaginary Companion By Age 7, Science Daily*. Available online at www.washington.edu/news/archive/id/6814 (accessed 9 November 2011).
9. Taylor, M. (2001) *Imaginary Companions and the Children Who Create Them* (2nd edn.). New York and Oxford: Oxford University Press.

10. Roby, A. and Kidd, E. (2008) The referential communication skills of children with imaginary companions, *Developmental Science*, 11(4): 531–40.
11. The classic study by Singer, J. and Singer, D. (1992) *The House of Make Believe: Play and the Developing Imagination*. Cambridge, MA: Harvard University Press.
12. Fair Play for Children (2004) *Play Action Guide: Inclusion in Play*. Bognor Regis: Fair Play for Children. Available online at www.fairplayforchildren. org/pdf/1200486561.pdf (accessed 29 January 2012).
13. Play Wales (2007) *Inclusive Play. Cardiff: Play Wales*. Available online at www.playwales.org.uk/downloaddoc.asp?id=233&page=67&skin=0 (accessed 18 January 2012) (p. 2).
14. John, A. and Wheway, R. (2004) *Can Play, Will Play: Disabled Children and Access to Outdoor Playgrounds*. London: National Playing Fields Association (p. 3).
15. Van Ausdale, D. and Feigin, J. (2001) *The First R: How Children Learn Race and Racism*. Lanham, MD: Rowman & Littlefield Publishers (p. 2).
16. Jane Lane and Haki Kapasi (2012): personal communication.
17. Douch, P. (2005) *The Busker's Guide to Inclusion*. Eastleigh: Common Threads. Also available online at www.commonthreads.org.uk (accessed 25 January 2012).
18. Papatheodorou, T. (2011) Play and the achievement of potential. In J. Moyles (ed.) *The Excellence of Play* (3rd edn.). Maidenhead: Open University Press.
19. Ward, F., Elliott, C. and Day, C. (2004) *I Want to Play Too*. London: Barnardos.
20. Whitebread, D. and Coltman, P. (2007) Developing children as self-regulated learners. In J. Moyles (ed.) *Beginning Teaching: Beginning Learning in Primary Education* (3rd edn.). Maidenhead: Open University Press.
21. Bodrova, E. and Leong, D. (2005) Self-regulation as a key to school readiness: how can early childhood teachers promote this critical competence? In M. Zaslow and I. Martinez-Beck (eds) *Critical Issues in Early Childhood Professional Development*. Baltimore, MD: Brookes Publishers.
22. Florez, I. (2011) *Developing Young Children's Self-regulation through Everyday Experience*. Available online at www.naeyc.org/files/yc/file/201107/Self-Regulation_Florez_OnlineJuly2011.pdf (accessed 18 January 2012) (p. 48).
23. Galinsky, E. (2010). *Mind in the Making: The Seven Essential Life Skills Every Child Needs*. NAEYC special edition. New York: HarperCollins.
24. David Whitebread (2012): personal communication.

J

Jargon of play

The majority of words associated with play can be found in various parts of this book: that is its purpose. Words like 'playful pedagogy,' cognitive development, free-flow play and playful dispositions are cited in different elements and references are given so that readers can follow these up in greater depth according to their need to know.

The other element of jargon is how the word 'play' is used in so many different contexts and, therefore, becomes confused in the minds of those who do not understand children's play for its powerful, developmental core. For example: play devil's advocate, play fair, foul play, make a play for, play the fool, play a trump card, play one's hand, go to a play and even the common sentences including 'It played a part in …' or 'They played host to …': all these use play in a way that is very different from that involved in the serious business of children's play and playful practitioners, although we hope to 'play a part' in children's development and learning – literally!

'Junk' (found/recycled materials) and play

This has always been one of my bugbears in relation to play! Really I dislike the term 'junk' but it is one used by so many people. Nowadays it is more eco-friendly to refer to 'found' or 'recycled' materials. Either way, children can always find a playful use for such things as egg boxes (growing seeds or sorting small items), cardboard tubes for experiments (rolling a car down a tube at various angles to see how incline makes a different to speed and distance), wallpaper ends for drawing and painting, and boxes of various shapes and sizes for making models. A creative and playful child (never mind the practitioners) will find a meaningful use for any of these items: therein, however, lies the nub of it. Children need to have chosen these items as part of their meaningful play rather than for them to be put out as a matter of course on Friday afternoons! Such materials need to be readily available all the time so that children who feel they want to model a shop as part of a shop play initiative have the materials and time to do so. Of course, it is useful too to talk with children about conservation and recycling as part of their material play.[1] Readers will need to make up their own minds about the use of food items; for example, pasta: my policy was always to use out-of-date goods so that they would not have been eaten anyway.

Practitioners are not immune from using covered recycled cans as pencil pots, and many playground items are now made with recycled materials including recycled structural plastic (RSP), which is also used for things like board-walks in play and public spaces. At The Proms in 2011, they even developed a whole orchestra and *played* the *1812 Overture* on created instruments made from recycled materials!

Reference

1. Sprung, B. (undated) *Helping Children Explore and Protect our Planet. Early Childhood Today (Scholastic).* Article available online at www.scholastic. com/teachers/article/helping-children-explore-protect-our-planet (accessed 4 February 2012).

K

Key Persons and play

Dorothy Selleck, whose work on Key Persons is well known, tells a story of
three babies in the care of their Key Worker and then reflects on the role of
the Key Person:

> She listens to each unique child in her group, watching all they do
> and say to tune into their play. She understands that the children's
> actions and expressions are the clues to their inner world of thoughts
> and feelings. She is uncertain but very knowledgeable about the ba-
> bies and sensitive to their play interests and communication. She
> is building on what she experienced yesterday in a physical bond of
> touching holding and watching. These babies are safe and learning in
> the professional intimacy of a relationship with a playful Key Person
> who is available and responsive to three different children in three
> different ways . . . .[1]

This well describes the role of the Key Person with babies and young
children. Using the Key Person approach means that each nursery or setting is
'enabling and supporting close attachments between individual children and
individual nursery staff.'[2] 'The Key Person approach recognizes that a baby or
young child may be distressed by differences and comforted by the familiar'[3]
and, therefore, close relationships and a known person to play with are at the
heart of the Key Person approach. It is she or he who will play closely with
the child and, as described above, will get to understand the developmental
needs of the child through close observation and emotional attachment to
those children. The Key Person, by being warm, sensitive and available to the

child, provides the security for that child to play and explore the setting, the materials and people this involves as well as providing a close link with the children's parents. In understanding the vital importance of play in its many guises, and adopting a playful approach themselves and conveying play's role in the child's development and well-being, the Key Person will enable the young children to flourish.

Note: A Key Worker, whose tasks are generally administrative and organizational, is not the same as a Key Person. Key Workers are often family support workers with a liaison role between different professionals or disciplines, making sure that services work in a co-ordinated way.

Kinaesthetic play

Most young children are what we might call 'kinaesthetic learners' as that means learning by physical play. But kinaesthetic learning goes further than that: it relates to the child who really does find it very difficult on the whole to stay still. We all know the child who even in very playful teaching situations keeps sliding off the chair or puts one leg on the chair and on the floor – we might insist that they try to 'sit still' but this is impossible for a truly kinaesthetic player and learner. Even in play, kinaesthetic learners are often easily distracted unless the play in which they are engaged integrates movement, both fine motor and gross motor.

In his theory of (nine) multiple intelligences, Gardner[4] identified bodily/kinaesthetic intelligence as the capacity to use one's whole body or parts of

Photograph K1 Learning about oneself from movement experiences

the body to solve a problem or make something. The kinaesthetic learner processes information mainly through touch and movement whereas auditory and visual learners learn respectively through hearing and sight. Of course, young children learn in all these ways but play provides the basic action and movement required for kinaesthetic learners.[5]

Music-making and dance are just two elements of kinaesthetic learning that we must retain in the early years curriculum for all children because of their creative elements but also for those who particularly learn and remember through kinaesthetic play. Being told something will mean little to kinaesthetic learners: they will remember something only if they have used bodily actions. This particularly applies to young children where handling and playing with objects will help them better to understand abstract concepts like quantity. Children (and adults) who learn through movement may well use gestures and facial expressions more than others in their play and other experiences. Practitioners can ensure when they playfully teach abstract concepts that they do so with movement; for example, throwing and catching balls while counting, or clapping/stamping when adding simple numbers together. Movement and rhythm play helps children to remember letter names and sounds.[6]

Children who are kinaesthetic learners will particularly enjoy play with all kinds of manipulative toys, construction sets, modelling materials like clay, physical experiments in which they are directly engaged like cooking, props for role play, learning outdoors, using bats, balls and other sports equipment, large-wheeled toys and music (to name but a few). There are close links here with outdoor physical play and health. Although not directed at young children, ideas for playful activities for kinaesthetic learners can be found in Jensen[7] and Smith.[8]

References

1. Dorothy Selleck (2012): personal communication.
2. Elfer, P., Goldschmied, E. and Selleck, D. (2003) *Key Persons in the Nursery: Building Relationships for Quality Provision.* London: David Fulton.
3. Mickelburgh, J. (undated) *Attachment Theory and the Key Person Approach.* Early Years Foundation Stage Forum. Available on line at www.eyfs.info/articles/article.php?Attachment-Theory-and-the-Key-Person-Approach-66 (accessed 17 January 2012).
4. Gardner, H. (1985) *Frames of Mind: The Theory of Multiple Intelligences.* New York: Basic Books.
5. Eberle, S. (2011) Playing with multiple intelligences: how play helps them grow, *American Journal of Play*, 4(1): 19–51.

6. Greenland, P. (2002) *Hopping Home Backwards: Body Intelligence and Movement Play*. Leeds: Jabadao.
7. Jensen, E. (2001) *Learning with the Body in Mind*. San Diego, CA: The Brain Store.
8. Smith, A. (2002) *Move it! Physical Movement and Learning*. New York: Network Continuum.

L

Language and communication play

The development of language and communications begins with a baby's very first playful moves when parents and carers talk to baby about things they are doing. We know that all children can learn any language up to around 12 months old but then the brain becomes attuned to the home language. Playing with this language – cooing, babbling, squealing – is the beginning of speech, language and communication, which will grow rapidly in the first five years. First words are playful repeats of what the young child has heard like milk, chair, biscuit and doggy. What is important in all language exchanges for young children is that speaking and listening is taking place with an interested 'other' in a meaningful, motivating and playful context, making language at home more relevant to children than that normally conducted in settings.[1]

There are two main language skills: receptive language (what a child 'receives' and understands) and expressive language (the words the child speaks). Both are known to be enhanced through play, especially pretend and socio-dramatic play.[2] Children learn language from playing with other children who have different experiences and vocabularies, and adults support play deliberately or inadvertently by, for example, describing play activities – 'That's a big, yellow teddy bear you're cuddling;' 'I can see you're enjoying cutting those juicy red apples' – and by asking open-ended questions: 'Why do you think your teddy is crying?.' Parents, family members and carers often provide such environments for children's play that are rich in language and, therefore, reinforce concepts and build on the children's play experiences. Adults can also interact with children in play when invited and carry on a (sensitive) dialogue within the play genre. Language has a clear emotional dimension: taking on different roles gives children licence to address feelings, anxieties and even fears and put these eventually into words, as can the use of puppets and other such toys. Playing with sounds and words – which children often do in play situations making deliberate 'mistakes' and roaring with laughter – supports friendships and the development of humour, and also teaches children that language is fun.

Play-rich environments reinforce and extend language skills in many different ways: socio-dramatic play encourages language development as children negotiate with each other, set up structures, explain games and interact in role with peers. Pretend play encourages language development as children negotiate roles, set up a structure, and interact in their respective roles.[3] All play provides a rich environment in which to practise language and communication skills.

From birth, all communication occurs within a socio-cultural context and language is strongly influenced by cultural and ethnic understandings. Play can support those children for whom English is a second language. 'Language is tied to culture and self-identity. Anything that reinforces an appreciation of a child's home language leads to a positive sense of self.'[4] Finding out how children play at home will enable practitioners to value different cultural approaches to play and vocabulary development.

Example L1

Oliver, an English speaker, is filling and pouring in the water tray. Close by, Anil, an Urdu speaker, is lifting water in a jug. Gradually, their actions merge and Oliver asks Anil 'Shall we do this together?' Anil does not understand but Oliver, through gestures and mime, gets his play partner. He tells Anil 'sand,' Anil tells Oliver 'rayt,' and so their play continues with both learning words and phrases in the two languages.

The development of *literacy* is also well supported in play:

> all forms of symbolic play ... signal the development of representational thought. The key importance of representational thought is that the child now is able to represent objects and events symbolically. Both literacy and symbolic play require the ability to use words, gestures or mental images to represent actual objects, events or actions.[5]

A study of 1–6-year-old children in the UK measured their capacity for symbolic play. Children were asked to substitute a teddy bear for an absent object and it was found that children who scored higher on tests of symbolic play had better language skills at all ages.[6]

Reading, but particularly telling stories and getting children to tell their own stories, enables them to play with ideas and be aware of their own language use.

Marian Whitehead, a renowned language and literacy expert, writes: 'A baby's earliest play with carers is all about communication: making eye contact, reading facial expressions and interpreting meanings. Language is meaningful sound. In vocal play infants explore the sounds, tunes and gestures of the languages used around them. Exploration of the sounds they can make and the things they can do with fingers, toes and toys, give babies and young children experiences of absorbed concentration and delight in the flow of exploratory play. Language and literacy, like play, are about having control of an activity, being motivated and remaining open to novelty, change and the fascinating nature of language and people, pictures and print.'[7]

Listening to children at play

There are two elements to 'listening' worthy of attention in this section: children listening and responding to each other during play experiences but also adults listening in to children at play. It is surprising how often practitioners have so much that they want to achieve *for* children that they do not take time to respect and listen *to* children. Many interventions in children's play literally interfere with rich language and thinking because a practitioner has not taken a moment to listen and reflect. The adult who asks 'What are you playing?,' however unwittingly, can end a meaningful play session. Listening to others is part of building sound relationships, trust and respect.[8]

Children in the twenty-first century are thought to have poorer listening skills and, therefore, poorer attention spans than in previous generations; this is often attributed to television and other media with conversations taking place in the context of continual noise.[9] The same can happen in play when children are so absorbed in what they are doing that they appear not to hear. We are all required to listen 'actively' because our mind actively engages in making meaning from what we hear: listening is actually quite hard work! Practitioners need to ensure that playful learning and teaching experiences make sense to young children and motivate them as worry about whether something is 'right' can be stressful and emotion then inhibits development.

Active listening is also about ensuring that what is said between practitioner and child is at child level both physically and intellectually: eye contact is important in group play situations particularly as each child needs to understand that adults are expecting them to listen. Using games that ensure each child has to listen to the one before are useful and playful: 'I went to the shops and I bought ...' is a classic game that most children love (and helps memory). Clapping response games are useful listening tools as is the musical freeze game where children 'freeze' when the music stops (for other ideas see note.[10]) But what about playful situations where the teacher has to listen to the children? Adults are so often busy hurrying children they do not remember that children take time to process information through hearing.[11] The game of passing round the teddy, where the holder is the speaker, means that adults and other children should listen to the holder of the teddy.

The skills everyone needs to be a good listener in play and life situations are:

- be patient and thoughtful: you may acquire new information about play or about the players;
- be open and honest in your listening to verbal exchanges in play: as adults, do not pretend to listen as children will always know!
- avoid interruption, intervention or interrogation: play has its own purposes that may not be explicable to anyone else!
- Show empathy and be attentive to the other person – really attentive – which will show in your body language;
- understand the other's need to communicate with you about the play or social context;
- understand that all play has value to the players.

Photograph L1 Listening to children

M

Making sense/meaning (see C = Cognitive play and learning and metacognition)
Manipulative play (see E = Exploratory/epistemic play)
Mastery play
Mathematics/numeracy (see C = Curriculum and play)
Memory (see C = Cognitive play and learning and metacognition)
Messy play
Modelling play (see A = Adult-initiated/guided play)
Moral development and play
Motivation and play
Multi-modality and play (see Introduction)

Mastery play

Example M1

When he was a toddler and into young childhood, my elder son had a toy called *Billy's Barrels*, a nesting toy like Russian dolls: each of six barrels fitted inside the next and finally, in the middle, there was a tiny 'Billy.' My son never tired of carefully putting Billy back in the tiniest barrel and building up the full set one inside the other. Then he would start all over again. In other respects he was very 'careless' with his toys, much preferring destruction to construction, but the mastery he felt in handling this particular toy was clearly very important to him.

This play with *Billy's Barrels* is a very common type of play among babies and young children. Even older children who are convincing themselves that they understand an object or situation will use repetition as a mastery strategy. To gain mastery, one needs perseverance and concentration during play and adults who understand that being able to master that action or take control over that object is really important to the young player. Mastery in adults is easily explained in relation to everyday actions like driving a car where, once mastered, you can drive without thinking about it and even have a conversation with your passenger. 'To be able to master tasks at any age requires that one has a belief in oneself that a task can indeed be mastered as a result of direct personal effort.[1]

Photograph M1 'Why does the water keep running away?'

Mastery can be achieved over objects or situations. Once something is mastered, children (and adults) can move on to innovate and extend their activity, the mastery having given them confidence, assurance and feelings of self-efficacy.[2] 'The internal excitement derived from ... mastery nurtures children's innate desire to learn. This passion and internalized sense of accomplishment is what motivates children's learning.'[3] 'The stronger the self-efficacy or mastery expectations, the more active the efforts.'[4] The child at mastery level play demonstrates a range of skilled motor movements and can simultaneously engage in pretend or symbolic play. In manipulating objects and materials with confidence, children also become more expert in expressing their ideas, thoughts and concepts. 'Recent research indicates that outdoor ... play may be essential to core mastery in children: it has been linked to improvements in cognitive, behavioral, and even physical functioning.'[5]

Practitioners need to organize play and learning activities so that children's experiences enable them to build confidence and mastery in what they do and, therefore, are energized to approach new learning situations.

Messy play

While as adults we might shy away from messy (sensory) play activities, if we work with young children then we have to be prepared for them to get messy through water, paint, clay, mud and other such materials. Why? Because it is through messy play that children really get their first-hand, sensory experiences of the textures, consistencies, sights, smells – very positive experiences despite the negative connotations for adults.[6] Messy play allows children to combine different materials in unique ways and make their own discoveries: for example, playing with dry sand, and sand and water in combination, and then relating this to the day on the beach. It allows kinaesthetic learners the opportunity they need for being physically involved.

Photograph M2 Messy play outdoors!

In messy play, children learn new vocabularies and gain new knowledge about everyday materials and experiences, as well as physical skills in handling, for example, dripping paint pots, and manipulating scissors and tools. Children's experimentation in messy play materials enables them to question why objects and materials behave in the way they do and open-ended questioning by adults enhances children's cognitive abilities. There is no 'right' way to play with messy materials; only things to be found out and file away for future reference in the developing brain. Engaging with children in their messy play shows them that the adults value the activity and can also provide an excellent opportunity for vocabulary extension and for learning about different children's co-ordination skills and even tolerances. It can also provide the stimulus for practitioners informally and playfully to teach children grouping and classifying, arranging items in order, identifying and matching items, understanding cause and effect, and observing and predicting.

Like many aspects of play, children's experiences of it will often be centred around settings and schools: busy parents or those from varied cultures are often reluctant to have messy play in the home or, indeed, to allow children messy opportunities outside.

> Children who are in the process of learning English as a second language can join in and use the materials with their peers because messy play does not rely on words ... children with special needs can use these open-ended materials in their own way and still be a part of the group.[7]

Messy play is infinite, open-ended and joyous for most children, but a nightmare for most adults, so do prepare the ground before messy play begins!

Moral development and play

Morals can be learned readily in play contexts because children make up their own 'rules' and break them frequently during all types of play! With young children, a sense of morals and ethics takes a long while to develop and is a complex developmental process.[8] Until about 8-years-old, children find it difficult (but not impossible) to see viewpoints other than their own. Until they can see others' perspectives (pro-social skills) they cannot handle the full scope of moral issues; that is, understanding tolerance, fairness, truth, integrity, justice, freedom of thought and respect for others.

With young children, feelings of empathy and acts of sharing can be present but are associated with and limited by the child's development. Playing with others in shared situations can help (but not force) a child's moral development. Morality in young children is mostly related to thinking about right and wrong, good and bad and even then, mainly in black-and-white terms, with some form of punishment as an outcome. When they will not share the toys, it is not because they are selfish in a moral sense, but because at that moment they feel that they need the toy more than the next child. In socio-dramatic play situations, however, children are often seen sharing playthings and doing so without conflict when, of course, the play context is under their control. Even if conflict arises, children can often sort out the situation for themselves in play without adult involvement (if we let them!)

While we can not make moral development happen in play or any other way, as practitioners we need to focus on behaviours a child will understand and enable them to construct an inner moral sense; one that grows intrinsically from a child's understanding rather than from externally imposed rules of conformity. Children must want to share toys or play spaces because they know inside that it is the right thing to do. Practitioners can support and develop children's understanding of morality through, for example, helping children to develop the classroom rules and talking with them about infringements. In observing different play sessions, teachers can talk with children about moral issues that have emerged and offer praise and encouragement for moral behaviours (as in Example M2). Games are also a useful way of eventually engendering in children understandings such as fairness, justice, rights and so on. A classic study shows that moral development can be facilitated if a child is regularly exposed to reasoning that is slightly higher than the level on which they are thinking.[9]

Example M2

Three 5-year-olds are playing a tag game where one child is 'it' and has to try and tag another who then becomes 'it' – and so the game continues. Reena accidentally trips up Alex, who cries 'You did that on purpose!' Cara runs over and helps to pick up Alex and rub his shoulder where he says it hurts. She tells Alex that Reena was 'only playing the game' and did not intend to hurt him. Reena nods and also touches Alex. She asks if Alex would now like to be 'it' (as a kind of compensation). Alex agrees and the game continues.

It is clear within this play that Cara understands the difference between intention and accidental harm and is able to pass on this concept to the others. Reena also understands a little about justice and fairness in that she offers Alex the chance to lead the game. This is typical of girls' play but not always of boys: when boys are confronted with a conflict they tend to argue or take their ball and go. On the other hand, girls will try to resolve the issue through compromise, although if that fails girls will generally change the activity rather than disband the group.[10]

Motivation and play

Some aspects of motivation have been incorporated in cognitive development and play. A few more specific things here will hopefully extend this topic.

Being motivated means wanting initially to participate in something: with play, this is innate in babies and young children so little else but mother nature is necessary!

Being motivated to persist with something can depend on two things: intrinsic and extrinsic motivation. When children are playing, they are doing it for purposes entirely within themselves (intrinsic motivation) and what they gain is interest, curiosity, pleasure and a sense of personal satisfaction and, sometimes, mastery. However, playful learning and teaching pedagogies may well encourage children to engage playfully but the reasons can become extrinsic: children are playing because that was the task set even if it is a playful one, and we all know that children want to please adults. If playing a game with the adult is what they want, children will happily go along with it in order to receive praise or, in some cases, stars and points systems.

Photograph M3 Motivation to learn by trial and error

If play and playful learning and teaching are paramount in classrooms and settings, it is unlikely that children will need extrinsic rewards to motivate them to learn. Extrinsic rewards like stars and other rewards imprint in the child the motivation to do the 'right thing' because of some external reward rather than because the child knows it is the proper way to behave or to play. In an extrinsic reward system, children can feel anxious if they do not get a star (and there are always children who miss out) and motivation is then diminished. If a child is stressed or anxious 'we stop learning dead in its tracks.'[11] Even superficial observation of play can show the extent to which play and playful activities involve and motivate children deeply.[12]

References

1. Starling, P. (2011) An investigation of unstructured play in nature and its effect on children's self-efficacy. Dissertation, *Scholarly Commons*, University of Pennsylvania (p. 10).
2. Pruett, K. (1999) *Me, Myself and I: How Children Build Their Sense of Self*. New York: Goddard Press.
3. Klein, T., Wirth, D. and Linas, K. (2004) Play: children's context for development. In D. Koralek (ed.) *Spotlight on Children's Play*. Washington, DC: NAEYC (pp. 28–25).
4. Bandura, A. (1977) *Social Learning Theory*. Alexandria, VA: Prentice Hall (p. 247).
5. Berman, L. (2007) *The Power of Play: What Children Learn by Unstructured Play*. Available online at www.ezinearticles.com/?The-power-of-play—what-childrenlearn-by-Unstructured-play&id=420404 (accessed 18 January 2012).
6. Duffy, B. (2007) *All About ... Messy Play*. London: Department for Children, Schools and Families. Available online at www.wsassets.s3.amazonaws.com/ws/nso/pdf/a5b16751ea9b55c5e83f455f5e54301f.pdf (accessed 27 January 2012).
7. Hands On Learning (2010) *Why is Messy Play Important?* Available online at www.ourhandsonlearning.com/messybenefits/php.
8. Edmiston, B. (2008) *Forming Ethical Identities in Early Childhood Play*. Abingdon: Routledge.
9. Kohlberg, L. (1981) *Essays on Moral Development, Vol. I: The Philosophy of Moral Development*. San Francisco, CA: Harper & Row.
10. Cyrus, V. (1993) *Experiencing Race, Class, and Gender in the United States*. Mountain View, CA: Mayfield Publishing Company.
11. Holt, J. (1991) *How Children Learn* (2nd edn.). New York: Merloyd Lawrence Delta (p. xv).
12. Golinkoff, R., Hirsh-Pasek, K., Berk, L.E. and Singer, D. (2009) *A Mandate for Playful Learning in Preschool: Presenting the Evidence*. New York: Oxford University Press.

N

Narrative play and story

Telling stories and playing with narratives about ourselves and our experiences are ways in which we build our notions of 'self,' who we are and our place in the world.[1] Storytelling has traditionally been something that practitioners do in early childhood settings but it is vitally important that children are given these opportunities too – after all, children with imaginary friends often make up stories about these friends and it seems a 'natural' thing for children to do in their pretend and socio-dramatic play. Narratives nowadays often come from popular culture and television characters as well as children's folklore and fairy-tales. Superhero play is mainly part of boys' narratives but also features rough and tumble play in which boys are generally more engaged than girls, whose play often involves themes of families and animals.

Story, in its broadest sense, describes an event or series of events (true or fictitious) with characters and a plot, whereas narrative describes how the story is told or recounted. Narrative is often oral but in young children's play it can encompass pictures, drawings or photographs. Narrative represents something in the child's life that has meaning and this is why it is so often connected with play. Practitioners can utilize narrative play to enrich children's experiences and provide an understanding of their own and other cultures.[2] Narrative play supports children's thinking and self-expression and interpreting narratives in different ways means children have to interpret the narrative in their own cultural context. Practitioners have traditionally written down children's narratives as personal stories or diaries, perhaps accompanied with drawings or photographs, and this is thought to be an excellent way of linking the play episode with literacy skills. Acting out children's own stories in a playful teaching and learning session might be a way of linking this child's life with that of others and developing empathetic relationships. There is a balance to be achieved between children's spontaneous pretend and socio-dramatic play episodes and that which is adult-initiated and guided.

Children who play well are often those who are good at narratives and can develop stories alone or with others: their narratives and stories can be about real or imagined events but include their experiences and ideas, and something of who we are.[3] 'Narrative play is a way of communicating with children using stories and narratives to share and make sense of life events.'[4] Quite young children can build upon each other's play themes and create several roles in elaborate play scenarios.[5]

Children dramatizing stories they have heard in their free play is vital to extending many different skills and understandings: folk-tales are often used in this way, with *Goldilocks and the Three Bears* a great favourite in my own reception class. The benefits of such stories and playing with and through them involve children in considerable cognitive demand: imagery, foresight, sequencing, vocalizing, listening and interpreting as well as the social relationships involved. When children are imagining something in their play, it entails a process of conscious thought and visualization, increasing brain activity and synaptic connections.

Avril Brock feels strongly that

> Stories in the mind (storying) is one of the most fundamental means of making meaning: children have a natural impulse to narrate stories as a means of making connections between what they are learning and what they already know ... Encouraging playful contexts rich in the language of story facilitates opportunities to understand, consolidate and explore vocabulary through activities and experiences. Observing children's story-play provides windows into children's minds and can provide insights into their metacognition; decision making and knowledge about story, language and learning.[6]

Natural world and play

This section is limited to play in the natural world outdoors: it has direct links with Forest School play. Playing outside in the big wide world and being involved with nature always attracts young children.[7] Playgrounds may offer limited scope for going 'wild' (in the best possible way). Wilder play – free play in open spaces – has been shown to have positive effects on socio-dramatic play, motor skills and, later, environmental awareness.[8]

Elements in the landscape are very appealing to children – construction can be on a large scale with pieces of wood, stones and branches (children can rarely do this in the usual playground situation) and there are places to hide, and rocks and trees to climb, feel and experience. Adults should aim to create a natural area for play, not a playground with a nature theme.[9] The outdoor world is much larger and 'is crucial because it is the primary mechanism through which children become acquainted with their environment.'[10] When two groups of children were compared – one in a natural landscape (a small wood) and the other in a traditional playground – the natural environment children were found to have significantly better motor fitness (particularly balance and co-ordination) than their peers in the traditional playground.[11]

Playing in the natural environment teaches children about spaces and places and brings them into contact with flowers and creatures that inhabit the natural spaces. It encourages children to care for the natural world and to experience the awe, wonder and spirituality associated with growth and seasonal changes. Sensitive adult intervention can ensure that in their play children begin to understand conservation and being eco-friendly. During the preschool years, it is important to help children discover what has been termed as their *ecopsychological self* – the child's natural sense of self in relation to the natural world.[12]

Natural world play can also include getting children to 'play' at gardening. Digging, sorting seeds, planting, watering and watching flowers and vegetables grow is a great source of delight for young children. In addition, settings and schools can, where space permits, create sensory gardens and allow the children quiet time to explore the sights, smells and textures of different plants.

Trisha Maynard observed children's play in the natural environment and noted:

> I was fascinated by the changes I observed in children's attitudes and behaviour when playing outdoors in a natural environment: these were children I barely recognised from my observations in the classroom . . . Outdoors, I have been struck by the relative complexity and sustained nature of children's play; their ability to cooperate and to engage, concentrate and pursue their own interests; their willingness to talk with adults and other children and to take risks . . . practitioners told me that such differences were particularly noticeable with children who 'struggled' emotionally or socially or with the learning of literacy and numeracy within the classroom context. When outdoors, many of these children, in one teacher's words 'came into their own' – they appeared more confident, motivated and capable, often taking on the role of leader in their play and investigations.[13]

Photograph N1 The wonder of growing your own seeds

Negotiation skills and play

The word negotiate means to confer with others and come to a mutual agreement. Play is a natural environment in which children develop negotiation skills. If you want a toy that another child has, you have to learn to negotiate or play with something else! If you want someone to play with you, you may have to allow them the role in your play that they demand; for example, if they want to be 'Daddy' in home area play. In developing negotiation skills, children are also learning resiliency, self-control and compromise.

Example N1

Emily and Sacha (both 3.5-years–old) are playing together with the large wooden blocks. Emily wants to build a house but Sacha wants to make a car like mummy's. At first, they each start to build their own construction and then realize that they are running out of blocks. Sacha takes one from Emily's construction and it looks as though Emily might start to cry. Then she looks at Sacha and says 'Are you my friend?' Sacha nods. 'Shall we build a house-car?' Emily says. The two then carry on building having negotiated a satisfactory compromise without adult intervention.

One study of the play of 2- and 3-year-olds demonstrates that even the youngest children can engage in negotiation during play episodes and that, in fact, negotiation regularly formed part of the children's play. In these negotiations, the children demonstrated invention, creativity, enthusiasm, industry, involvement and problem-solving strategies. One conclusion of the study is that:

> In negotiations that stem from agreement – in other words the children are agreed that they will share their play – the play features efforts by the children to understand their friends' perspective as well as playful development of the imagination. However, negotiations arising from disagreement involve play that is more about power, domination and manipulation.[14]

During play episodes, children learn to express their ideas and their rationales: reasons they must be responsive to the ideas of other children. Compromise and negotiation skills help children build upon each other's ideas for mutual enjoyment. Practitioners can significantly help children to extend their negotiating skills by:

- giving children ownership of and independence in their play and respecting their views and feelings;
- helping them to understand a repertoire of negotiation skills such as persuasion and alternative choices;
- modelling positive negotiation in practice with children in their play: 'we have 30 minutes before lunchtime – would you like a story or time to play?' 'Why do you make that choice?'
- settling disputes over playthings without blaming individuals: showing both sides of the argument;
- talking with both children who are upset because one has not succeeded in negotiating their wants, getting each to explain how it feels and what they think of the situation.

Everyone can learn to negotiate: even very young babies show the beginnings of negotiation and reciprocity during playful interactions with adults to whom they are attached.[15]

References

1. Harrett, J. (2002) Young children talking: an investigation into the personal stories of Key Stage One infants, *Early Years: Journal of International Research and Development*, 22(1): 19–26.

2. Rettig, M. (1995) Play and cultural diversity, *The Journal of Educational Issues of Language Minority Students*, 15: 1–9.
3. Cattanach, A. (2007) *Narrative Approaches in Play with Children*. London: Jessica Kingsley.
4. Cattanach, A. (op. cit.: p. 21).
5. Feuer, C., Jefferson, D. and Resick, P. (2001) Play patterns and gender. In J. Worrell (Editor-in-Chief) *Encyclopedia of Women and Gender*, Vol. 2. London: Academic Press.
6. Avril Brock (2012): personal communication.
7. Herbert, T. (2008) Eco-intelligent education for a sustainable future life. In I. Pramling Samuelsson and Y. Kaga (eds) *The Contribution of Early Childhood to a Sustainable Society*. Paris: UNESCO.
8. Lindstrand, P. (2005) *Playground and Outdoor Play: A Literature Review*. Stockholm: Stockholm International Toy Research Centre (pp. 59–68).
9. Design Principles for Nature Play Spaces (2009) *Omaha, Nebraska: Green Hearts: Institute for Nature in Childhood*. Available online at www.greenheartsinc.org/uploads/Green_Hearts_Design_Principles_for_Nature_Play_Spaces.pdf (accessed 21 January 2011).
10. Valentine, G. (2004) *Public Space and the Culture of Childhood*. London: Ashgate (p. 74).
11. Fjortoft, I. (2001) The natural environment as a playground for children: the impact of outdoor play activities in pre-primary school children, *Early Childhood Education Journal*, 29(2): 111–17.
12. Phenice, L. and Griffore, R. (2003) Young children and the natural world, *Contemporary Issues in Early Childhood*, 4(2): 167–78.
13. Trisha Maynard (2012): personal communication.
14. Alvestad, T. (2010) Preschool relationships – young children as competent participants in negotiations. PhD thesis, University of Gothenburg, Faculty of Education.
15. David, T., Gouch, K., Powell, S. and Abbott, L. (2003) *Birth to Three Matters: A Review of the Literature*. London: DfES Research Brief 444. Available online at www.niched.org/docs/Bibliographic%20assessment%20example.pdf (accessed 20 January 2012).

O

Object play

Object play is literally play with objects of different kinds for different purposes. The nub of object play, however, is that once children reach age 2–3 they begin to use objects to represent something else: a piece of cloth can become a baby or a block can become a spoon or a gun – object substitution. Babies and infants first have to learn 'object permanence', which means recognizing that anything which is hidden – be it parent or toy – still exists even if you can't see it. This occurs usually before the first birthday – as with all things to do with children, as each is unique, so is the stage of development. Infants and toddlers require plenty of manipulation of objects to develop brain circuitry.

Children as young as 3–4-years-old can remember over a play episode what the object was intended to represent even though, in the meantime, it might have been changed by the children to represent something else! 'Investigations into children's ability to coordinate multiple perspectives in [object] pretence beyond such implicit perspective tracking abilities have revealed clear competence in four-year-olds.' The researchers also suggest that: 'by age 3, children understand that an object can have multiple pretend identities'.[1] Similar research has shown that 'young children demonstrate pretence comprehension more competently through their pretend actions than their capacity to correctly answer verbal questions'[2] showing yet again that, in their play, children are able to express more competence than in oral exchanges with adults.

Object substitution is an important element in children's play because it means that children are not dependent on toys – any objects (such as those in treasure baskets, and sticks and stones in nature play) can become tools for

Table O1 Development of object play

Birth–1.5 years	Use senses to explore objects. By the end of this period, object permanence is established
1.5–2 years	Relational object play continues but, by the end of this period, children can substitute one object for another and begin to pretend that the same object has two different identities
2–3 years	Pretence play is developing and, by the end of this period, children can talk about multiple pretend identities for objects in play sequences
4+ years	children understand different pretence perspectives held by others and remember their substitutions

play. Understanding object substitution is also vital in later life; for example, pieces of paper represent money.

The practitioner's role is mainly to assess the levels of development shown by children in object play and recognize progress. Babies and infants need the stimulus of the provision of a wide range of objects for exploration and, as children get older, the freedom to engage with each other in object substitution play.[3] Adults can join in and 'drink' the cup of 'hot chocolate' provided to them in the home area and extend children's vocabulary by talking about the taste and temperature.

Outdoor play

Outdoor play should be about enjoying whatever the weather throws at us – rain and snow, for example, are a constant source of pleasure to children yet few UK settings encourage play in those conditions. Boots, waterproofs and umbrellas at the ready, young children should spend as much time outdoors as possible as this is known to be good for their health, weight and general well-being. In the outdoor play and learning environment children can practise emerging physical skills, experience the joy of movement and the pleasure of greater independence, and burn calories!

Play theorists widely argue the particular importance of outdoor play, which is associated with benefits such as acquiring life skills and improving children's emotional and academic development.[4] Much of what children do during outdoor play, including the sharing of folk culture, making choices and developing rules for play, involves the development of social skills.[5] It seems self-evident that 'outdoor play experiences contribute to children's physical development, in particular to motor development. Less obvious is the learning that happens as children test their strength, externally and internally: How high can I climb? Why do I breathe differently when I run? Am I brave enough to jump from this platform?'[6]

Settings that ensure 'free-flow' play, where children move independently and freely, ensure more physically active play among the children.[7] Sitting for more than 10 minutes at a time is known to reduce our awareness of physical and emotional sensations and increases tiredness, the result of which is reduced concentration and discipline problems.[8] The rationale for demanding children sit *more*, therefore, is counter-intuitive both to what the research shows and to what we know about children. Children who have little opportunity to be active during the school day rarely compensate during after-school hours (see R = Risk). Yet advances in brain research show that most of the brain is activated during physical activity.[9] In Finland, playtime is an important part of the daily schedule and children return to classrooms refreshed and ready to learn; indeed, Finnish children aged 7–8 score higher on reading tests[10] despite starting reading much later than UK children.

Photograph 01 The benefits of outdoor play

Young children do not process information as quickly as older children meaning they benefit especially by breaks from seated activities: therefore, the outdoor learning environment should not try to replicate the classroom but be an experience that is differently challenging. As Angela Anning explains:

> I worry about the concept of 'outdoor classrooms' being misinterpreted. I shudder when I see words stuck to objects outside – ladder, shed, climbing frame, plant – to improve 'literacy' or number lines and grids everywhere to improve 'numeracy.' I have no problems with labels like Storage Shed or Workshop or tape measures which connect to the real world. I want outdoor play to give children opportunities to build dens out of poles and tarpaulins and make aeroplanes out of boxes. I want them to be able to grow their own vegetables and plants and dig in real mud. I want them to be able to splash around in water and build dams and castles in big sandpits. I want them to be able to run and jump and hop and skip and throw things around. I want them to be able to dance and make loud music and paint on big pieces of paper without worrying about the mess. I want them to be able to curl up under a tree or in a den with a book. I don't want more of the same of 'classroom' drilling in literacy and numeracy.[11]

Ownership

Ownership is an important concept in children's play: if children do not 'own' the activity then it hardly constitutes play at all! Ownership is related to deep involvement and intense concentration, so play – which is, by definition, self-chosen – allows children deep involvement and the need to carry on with the play for as long as deemed necessary. But, as I have indicated elsewhere, play can readily be hijacked by adults and then the play ownership ceases, often to the great distress of the children. This can happen quite unintentionally on the part of the practitioner: even when the adult thinks that they are engaging with play in the hospital area as a 'patient,' one question out of place can take away the ownership, especially something like 'What do you want me to pretend next?' Even this innocent statement shows children that the adult is not really absorbed in the play and has not fully taken on the required role.

There is great value in a 'learning–teaching environment where children play and learn together in creative, investigative and problem-solving ways, where they can take ownership of and responsibility for their own learning and where their emotional and imaginative needs are met.'[12] We need, however, to find out what children think about the play experiences in which they are involved: checking children's perceptions – and whether they perceive they have ownership – is an important aspect of listening to

Table O2 Children, ownership and playful learning[13]

Using children's perceptions to exploit playfulness	
Space and constraint	In a structured setting children often learn that work occurs at a table and play in any location. Where such a boundary does not exist, children are more able to feel ownership in a range of activities
Teacher presence	When children are unused to adult involvement in play they often use this as a defining characteristic. Consequently an activity loses its play status (and ownership) when an adult is present. Use of this cue can be prevented if children frequently experience adult engagement in all play activities
Positive affect	Encouraging positive affect in a range of play activities can maximize learning by evoking a playful approach that offers ownership to the children
Skill development	Increased emphasis on skill development and attainment reduces feelings of playfulness and ultimately ownership. It is, therefore, important to emphasize playful processes over outcomes
Choice and control	Children may approach activities more playfully when they perceive choice and ownership (even if this is engineered!)

children which may lead to practitioners questioning their own assumptions and beliefs about play and its value to children and their learning. Research outlined in Table O2 indicates some ways in which practitioners can exploit ownership and playfulness in children's activities and experiences.

One early pioneer of early childhood play is adamant that children know what they are doing in their play; they know what matters to them and why.[14] We should respect this through ensuring that ownership of their play and learning is given to the children as often as possible. Children's ownership also raises issues of power relations: children are usually subordinate to adults but, in play, they can feel the exhilaration of being 'powerful' and in control of that play at that time.

References

1. Wyman, E., Rakoczy, H. and Tomasello, M. (2009) Young children understand multiple pretend identities in their object play, *British Journal of Developmental Psychology*, 27(2): 385–404 (pp. 386, 399).

2. Rakoczy, H., Tomasello, M. and Striano, T. (2006) The role of experience and discourse in children's developing understanding of pretend play actions, *British Journal of Developmental Psychology*, 24(2): 305–35.
3. Hughes, A. (2010) *Developing Play for the Under Threes*. London: Routledge.
4. Ginsburg, K. (2006) *The Importance of Play in Promoting Healthy Child Development and Maintaining Strong Parent–Child Bonds*. Washington, DC: American Academy of Pediatrics.
5. Bishop, J. and Curtis, M. (eds) (2001) *Play Today in the Primary School Playground*. Maidenhead: Open University Press.
6. Hewes, P. and MacEwan, G. (2005) *Let the Children Play: Nature's Answer to Early Learning*. Early Childhood Learning Knowledge Centre. Available online at www.tinyurl.com/an46p8 (accessed 20 January 2012) (p. 4).
7. Brady, L., Gibb, J., Henshall, A. and Lewis, J. (2008) *Play and Exercise in Early Years: Physically Active Play in Early Childhood Provision*. Available online at www.culture.gov.uk/images/research/Playresearch2008 (accessed 25 January 2012).
8. Pellegrini, A. and Bohn, C. (2005) The role of recess in children's cognitive performance and school adjustment, *Educational Researcher*, 34(1): 13–19.
9. Shonkoff, J. and Phillips, D. (eds) (2000) *From Neurons to Neighborhoods: The Science of Early Childhood Development*. Washington, DC: National Academy Press.
10. Alvarez, L. (2005) Educators flocking to Finland, land of literate children, *New York Times*, 9 April (p. A4).
11. Angela Anning (2011): personal communication.
12. Broadhead, P. (2006) Developing an understanding of young children's learning through play: the place of observation, interaction and reflection, *British Educational Research Journal*, 32(2): 191–207 (p. 192).
13. Howard, J. (2002) Exploiting playfulness to maximise learning in the early years classroom. Paper presented at the BERA Conference, University of Exeter, 12–14 September.
14. Lowenfeld, M. (1991) *Play in Childhood*. London: MacKeith Press (first published in 1935, London: Gollancz).

P

Parallel play (see S = Social development and play)
Parents and play
Persistence (see M = Motivation and play)
Photography and play
Physical play
Planning for play/playfulness
Power relations and play (see O = Ownership)
Practice play (see M = Mastery play)
Praise (see M = Motivation and play)
Pretend play (see I = Imaginative play/imaginary friends)
Problem solving (see C = Cognitive play and learning and metacognition)

Parents and play

Play is valued differently among different cultures – adult attitudes are often one of indifference.[1] Western parents often support their children's play, especially mothers, as being good for children's education and learning but it is nevertheless common for parents to think that play is only an early stage of development that should very soon be replaced with educational 'work.' One study found that parents in the UK, the US and France would prefer their children to be involved in organized activities rather than free play during their free time but most parents in Japan and Germany would encourage free play.[2] Yet parental engagement in play and playful experiences is known to have a significant impact on, for example, the cognitive development and language skills of the child[3] as well as their social skills and building of relationships.

Parents setting aside time to play with children is thought to be vital and to do this adult roles must be left behind for a more balanced relationship.[4] This is difficult for some parents, particularly those from poorer backgrounds. The *Millennium Cohort Study*[5] showed big differences in cognitive development between children from rich and poor backgrounds at the age of 3, which had widened by age 5. 'This suggests that policies to improve parenting skills and home learning environments cannot, in isolation, eliminate the cognitive skills gap between rich and poor young children.'[6] Some of this was attributed to less advantageous 'early childhood caring environments,' which includes parents' interest in playing with their children.

Parents may well need support from practitioners to understand the value of play to their young children and the need to 'make time and opportunities for one-to-one interaction, talking and listening with babies and young children ... and playing.'[7] Research suggests that the most creative children are those who have adult involvement in their play: 'the richest play occurs when adults take an active role ... When children play with adults, they display higher levels of language and problem solving skills than when playing with their peers.'[8] Numerous studies have shown the importance of parents and language play to children's later literacy achievements.

Photography and play

Increasingly, practitioners and children are using photography to highlight the benefits of play-based learning in settings. Photograph diaries, portfolios, learning journals and profiles (under various guises) are now common in a range of settings and schools, and these provide evidence for parents and others involved in early education that children are learning through their photographed and documented play. The camera is a great way to authenticate children's development over time.

Photograph P1 Taking photos is great fun – and useful

Using a camera motivates even the youngest and can engage children in researching their own play and reflecting on it,[9] as well as involvement in developing their own learning diaries. Both children and practitioners can use video and photography for research purposes; for example, children can be encouraged to talk about their play activities through reflecting on photographs previously taken. Practitioners can use video and photography to analyse how children use the various playthings and play areas available to them in the setting or classroom and to monitor individual children's play choices and relationships.

A word of caution is needed: any photographs used outside the context of one's own settings is subject to data restrictions and protocols to which one must adhere. And, of course, children should be asked about their preferences for sharing their photographs and diaries.

Physical play

Physical play is linked, as we have seen elsewhere, to children's growing physical competence and health. Most young children are only too keen to 'let off steam' and be physical, playing on large-wheeled toys or using climbing frames and other large play equipment (locomotor play). The development of muscle control is the first step in children's physical maturation and they do this through playing with objects and people. Gradually, co-ordination develops in a sequence of gross and fine motor skills something like this:

1 Large to small: large muscles develop in the neck, body, arms and legs before the small muscles in the fingers, hands, wrists and eyes – children can walk before they can make marks.
2 Head to toe: babies can hold up their heads long before they can walk.
3 Centre to outer body: muscles around the centre of the body develop earlier and stronger than muscles in the hands and feet.

The prime time for physical development and physical play is between birth and 12 years of age. Playful, physical interaction with the world is a critical part of growing up and is key to both gross-motor and fine-motor skills development. Just think of ball play: a baby, even with a soft ball, can hold it and roll it away: by the time she is 12 months old, she can either crawl or walk to fetch the ball and make an effort at throwing. Towards the end of this period the pincer grip will develop and now the child can hold a small ball between forefinger and thumb and can also drop the ball into a box. Within another year, she can throw the ball to another person (if not accurately!) and by 3-years-old she may be able to catch with her arms. By 4-years-old kicking the ball has become very easy and by 5-years-old throwing and catching is mainly co-ordinated. Such an amazing refinement of skills over these few short years is indicative of the power of physical play. Alongside these gross motor skills, the child will gradually learn fine motor skills – for example, the ability to hold a crayon and paintbrush – but it will be some time before the fine motor skills are refined enough to be able to form letters and numbers accurately. Balance and co-ordination will also emerge through climbing, running, chasing, constructional toys and such like.

Photograph P2   Co-ordination in physical play

While engaged in gross motor physical play, a child is likely to 'encounter opportunities for decision making that stimulate problem-solving and creative thinking … Learning … that play and movement relieves stress and enhances mood may help children sustain physical activity patterns over their lifetime.'[10] It is thought that moderate and vigorous gross-motor activities provide the brain with its chief energy source, glucose: such activities increase blood flow, which feeds the brain and enhances brain connectivity.[11]

Planning for play/playfulness

Planning for play/playfulness is a contradiction in terms: it not possible to plan for a process that is spontaneous, self-chosen and under the ownership of the child. What practitioners can plan for – through observation of children's interests, cultures and sustained play episodes – is provision of whatever material or human resources are needed to extend and elaborate the children's play.

Practitioners may also want to make plans for brief periods of playful learning and teaching[12] ensuring that they 'maintain playfulness through: being outgoing, energetic and active, in their presentation of material, preserving a light-hearted tone, leaving room for some spontaneity.'[13] It is suggested that the 'playful approach and attitude that is taken [by practitioners] ... rather than the play act itself which is beneficial to learning,'[14] although other researchers suggest: 'The construct of playfulness comprises the internal qualities brought to the activity by the players themselves ... to understand the nature of playfulness, it is necessary to understand how players perceive their activities ... if children use teacher presence when making judgements about play, then they are less likely to approach an activity playfully when there is teacher involvement.'[15]

In their planning, practitioners can and should: consider the physical spaces suitable for different types of play and how play fulfils the intended curriculum outcomes and the cultural/ethnic backgrounds of the children; provide accessories for play (e.g. dressing-up materials); and decide how play episodes can fit into the daily timetable. Planning is making choices with particular intentions in mind (e.g. learning and development). All planning undertaken will also be dependent on any externally imposed curricula while bearing in mind that these are only guides and children need a wide range of motivating experiences and infinite ways of expressing themselves through their play. Planning for play will be better achieved if parents are involved and informed about the importance of play[16] and its powerful learning potential for young children. Vital to planning is that children are not rushed through activities but are given time to sustain their play episodes and build on them through planned adult support where relevant.

Children are our best guides to all planning: if the play environment 'stimulates and inspires children's imaginations, they can provide ... the practitioner with rich material on which [to] base planning and think about appropriate resources.'[17] It is also believed that 'Engaging children in planning and reflection makes them more than good actors following prescribed roles. It turns them into artists and scientists who make things happen and create meaning for themselves and others ... when children plan, carry out, and review their own learning activities, their behavior is more purposeful and they perform better on language and other intellectual measures.'[18]

References

1. Rossie, J.-P. (2005) *Toys, Play, Culture and Society: An Anthropological Approach With Reference to North Africa and the Sahara.* Stockholm: Stockholm International Toy Research Centre.

2. Lego Learning Institute (2003) *The Changing Face of Children's Play Culture.* Slough: The Lego Learning Institute.

3. Dickinson, D. (ed.) (2001) *Beginning Literacy with Language: Young Children Learning at Home and at School.* Baltimore, MD: Paul Brookes Publishing.

4. Donaldson, F. (2001) In the company of children, *PlayRights*, 23(3): 11–14.

5. Bradshaw, J. and Holmes, J. (2004/5) *Millennium Cohort Study Briefing 3: Child Poverty In the First Five Years of Life.* London: Centre for Longitudinal Studies, University of London. Available online at: www.cls.ioe.ac.uk/downloads/03_briefing_web.pdf (accessed 20 January 2012).

6. Joseph Rowntree Foundation (2010) *The Importance of Attitudes and Behaviour for Poorer Children's Educational Attainment.* Available online at: www.jrf.org.uk/sites/files/jrf/poorer-children-education-summary.pdf (accessed 4 February 2012).

7. Joseph Rowntree Foundation (ibid.)

8. The National Toy Council (undated) *Intergenerational Play.* London: The National Toy Council. Available online at: www.btha.co.uk/dynamic/documents/ntcleaflets/intergenerational_play.pdf (accessed 20 January 2012).

9. Burke, C. (2005) Play in focus: children researching their own spaces and places for play, *Children, Youth and Environments*, 15(1): 27–53.

10. Burdette, H. and Whitaker, R. (2005) Resurrecting free play in young children looking beyond fitness and fatness to attention, affiliation, and affect, *Archives of Pediatrics and Adolescent Medicine*, 159(12): 46–50 (p. 46).

11. Woodfield, L. (2004) *Physical Development in the Early Years*. London: Continuum. See also Liddle, T. and Yorke, L. (2003) *Why Motor Skills Matter: Improving Your Child's Physical Development to Enhance Learning and Self-Esteem*. New York: McGraw-Hill.

12. Moyles, J. (2010) Practitioner reflection on play and playful pedagogies. In J. Moyles (ed.) *Thinking about Play: Developing a Reflective Approach.* Maidenhead: Open University Press.

13. Walsh, G., Sproule, L., McGuinness, C. and Trew, K. (2011) Playful structure: a novel image of early years pedagogy for primary school classrooms, *Early Years: An International Journal of Research and Development*, 31(2): 107–19, (p. 112).

14. McInnes, K., Howard, J., Miles, G. and Crowley, K. (2011) Differences in practitioners' understanding of play and how this influences pedagogy and children's perceptions of play, *Early Years: International Journal of Research and Development*, 31(2): 121–33 (p. 123).

15. Howard, J., Belling, W. and Rees, V. (2002) Eliciting children's perceptions of play and exploiting playfulness to maximise learning in the early years classroom. Paper presented at the BERA Conference, University of Exeter, 12–14 September (pp. 4, 12).

16. Tassoni, P. and Hucker, K. (2005) *Planning Play in the Early Years* (2nd edn.). Oxford: Heinemann.
17. Canning, N. (2011) Exploring the possibilities of the play environment. In N. Canning (ed.) *Play and Practice in the Early Years Foundation Stage.* London: Sage Publications (p. 96).
18. Epstein, A. (2003) *How Planning and Reflection Develop Young Children's Thinking Skills. Beyond the Journal.* Young Children on the Web. Available online at www.journal.naeyc.org/btj/200309/Planning&Reflection.pdf (accessed 12 January 2012) (pp. 2, 8)

Q

Quality play

Quality play is about children's quality of life and rights: children have the right to play enshrined in law (see U = United Nations Convention on the Rights of the Child). It is about children having high-quality playtime free from adult constraints, quality time with peers and quality in the provision made for their play in settings, schools, at home and in the wider environment. Quality play experiences are ones in which children guide and control the play situation and achieve ownership of it. Quality is about provision of appropriate resources for play both indoors and out. The quality of playfulness is one all practitioners need if they are to play with and care effectively for all young children. Local authority services for children's community-based play are aspiring to quality through improved play spaces and playwork training.

While quality is open to interpretation,[1] we all know what it looks like when we see it, just as we know when children are experiencing quality play on their own terms. Self-evaluation can provide practitioners with insights into the quality of their play and learning provision for young children.[2]

Some researchers are concerned that 'the increasing emphasis on accountability [has] led to a corresponding decline in the general understanding of the important contribution that high-quality play ... can make to children's cognitive development in the early years.'[3] And there is also the issue of changes in childhood which have occurred in the last 10 years or so which is thought to undermine the quality of children's play both inside and outside settings and schools. The teaching of 'basics' at younger and younger ages can mean that even the youngest children are denied quality play experiences.

Photograph Q1 What constitutes quality in children's play experiences?

Parents, too, are expected to spend quality time with their children and research has shown that some of the best parent–child interactions occur in play episodes but also when doing routine activities (playfully!) such as preparing meals, shopping and engaging in hobbies.[4]

Questioning

Children asking questions is quite common in certain contexts and, certainly, children being *asked* questions in and about their play is very common indeed. Good practitioners extract information from children about their play sensitively and playfully. But many questions asked by adults of children are quite closed 'What colour is that train?' 'Have you got a doll?' These closed questions do not expand the child's learning and understanding or reveal their play experiences to the practitioner. They do little to inform the practitioners of the child's development either.

The heart of sensitive yet effectively probing questions is to ask *genuine* open-ended questions: things to which you really want an answer that you do not already know! 'How can I make this better?' 'What should we do now?' 'We've put all the things in the shop: what shall we do now?' make for genuine interaction between adult and child, rather than the adult asking questions about colours and shapes of toys to which it is obvious to the child that the adult already knows the answer. Such open-ended questions are integral to children's thinking skills, creativity, problem solving and cognitive growth. Neither is there any worry on the part of the child that they will not get the answer 'right.'

Questions can ask about feelings or about concrete aspects of play; for example, 'What is it like when you're squeezing the dough?' as opposed to 'How does the dough feel when you squeeze it?' – both open, but both eliciting different kinds of response. Whatever the questions directed at children, they need to have meaning and be related to play and other direct experiences in children's lives. Such questions should also help children with their meta-cognition so that they begin to understand their own playful learning processes.[5]

Children themselves should be encouraged to generate questions (and not just those of the 'why' variety!) in order to gather needed information so that they can use the information gained productively: it is known that children tap into their existing conceptual knowledge when they raise questions. The ability to ask questions is a powerful tool that allows children to gather information they need in order to learn about the world and solve problems they experience in it.[6] 'A classroom where questions are celebrated and modelled will create an ethos of creative and critical thinking.'[7]

Practitioners may want to question themselves – or question each other within the team – about their learning in the setting: about the ways in which the children play and the adults' playful interactions, the quality of the resources, and what they have learned to enable high-quality play provision the next day or week.

Quiet play

Children occasionally need quiet time and quiet places to play. As with adults, quiet time enables the child to absorb, digest, think, reason and just have peace and calm (for a while). Quiet time does not require much physical energy and may not require much space. Quiet play can be looking at pictures or books, sitting out in the natural world, listening to music and playing with imaginary friends. Quietness offers time to reflect on play experiences and to be comfortable with yourself and perhaps a friend. Quiet play may involve toys or could be a solitary child watching others – observer play. Quiet play is sometimes very independent play as the child absorbs themselves in making a discovery or exploring, say, a threading toy, small world figures or a flower.

Quiet spaces should be created both indoors and outdoors.[8] Reading and writing areas plus role-play spaces can all provide indoor quiet play areas: the quiet area normally has carpeting, comfortable chairs and pillows, a low bookshelf for books and some soft toys. Green quiet spaces in outdoor and Forest School play can be created with sticks and twigs. Tents (made around tables with sheets of fabric) and other home-made structures can provide quiet places readily and cheaply. Blankets and cushions can help children sit quietly and calmly. Sometimes it is good to have a seat too. Children are naturally drawn to small, comforting spaces where they can be alone or with one or two others. If quiet spaces are a part of the available play space, children will naturally seek these out to calm down, or just to spend a short time being themselves. Any adult interruption, even for a moment, can break the quiet, magic spell, so much sensitivity is needed around quiet play.

References

1. Dahlberg, G., Moss, P. and Pence, A. (2006) *Beyond Quality in Early Childhood Education and Care: Languages of Evaluation*. London: Routledge.
2. Mohamed, C. and Lissaman, S. (2009) *Valuing Quality in the Early Years: Improving the Quality of Provision in All Early Years Settings*. London: Featherstone Education/A&C Black.
3. Bergen, D. (2002) The role of pretend play in children's cognitive development, *Early Childhood Research and Practice*, 4(1). Available online at www.ecrp.uiuc.edu/v4n1/bergen.html (accessed 22 January 2012).
4. Ginsburg, K. (2007) The importance of play in promoting healthy child development and maintaining strong parent-child bonds, *Pediatrics*, 119(1): 182–91.
5. Alexander, R. (2004) *Towards Dialogic Teaching: Rethinking Classroom Talk*. Cambridge: Dialogos.
6. Choinard, M. (2007) *Children's Questions: A Mechanism for Cognitive Development*. Hoboken, NJ: Wiley-Blackwell.
7. Macro, C and McFall, D. (2004) Questions and questioning: working with young children, *Primary Science Review*, 83: 4–6.
8. Bullard, J. (2010) *Creating Environments for Learning: Birth to Age Eight*. Upper Saddle River, NJ: Pearson Education.

R

Recapitulative play

Associated with risk-taking, recapitulative play is relatively 'primitive' play that allows the child to explore ancestry, history, rituals, stories, rhymes and cultural norms. It enables children to access the play of earlier human evolution.[1]

Reflecting on play

Reflecting on play has arisen in a number of entries so this is short. All those in settings should ensure that adults *and* children are reflecting on their play and what they learn through playing and observing play. Practitioners need also to reflect on the playfulness of their approaches with children – we all know that if it feels like play to the children, their motivation and enthusiasm are increased and perpetuated.

Most early childhood practitioners recognize the importance of developing memory skills in young children. Teachers might ask children to remember play activities occurring earlier in the day or to recall an event earlier in the week. Reflection, however, is more than memory or a rote recitation of completed activities. Reflection is *remembering with analysis*. When we engage children in reflection, we encourage them to go beyond merely reporting what they have done. We also help them become aware of what they learned in the process, what was interesting, how they feel about it, and what they can do to build on or extend the experience.

Reflection also consolidates knowledge so it can be generalized to other situations, thereby leading to further prediction and evaluation: this applies to all those doing the reflecting. Thus planning and reflection, when they promote active learning, are part of an ongoing cycle of deeper thought and thoughtful application.[2]

Risk/risky play

Risk/risky play is about young children pushing themselves just that little bit further in order to do something they have not done before but would like to do.

Photograph R1   You can do it, Ben!

Example R1

Ben, aged 20 months, is at the top of the slide. He looks down and clearly feels the ground looks a long way away. He hesitates and his grandma says, 'You can do it, Ben!' Ben still hesitates as another child pushes past him and launches herself down the slide. Having watched the girl's actions, Ben sits down and pushes himself down the slide. 'Grandma, I did it!' he exclaims at the bottom and runs up the steps to go down again (and again, and again . . .).

Example R2

Issy, aged 6, is paddling in a stream: her family watches from the bank. She sees a rope hanging over the edge of the stream from a tree and scrambles up the bank. Fortunately, she has a swimsuit on because she immediately grabs the rope, pulls it backwards and launches herself out and over the water and then lets go of the rope and splashes down.

Photograph R2 Taking risks in water

These children are not alone, as many of us can attest, in seeking the thrill of taking risks.[3] Even quite young children soon enjoy climbing on everything in sight, jumping from heights, running fast, being hung upside by trusted adults and thrown up into the air. This helps them develop co-ordination and control and endorses self-efficacy.

Both the children in the examples are taking risks at their own levels and testing themselves in the wider world. They also test new ideas, solve problems, show resourcefulness, invention and creativity. 'Risky play becomes the ground where children can actualise their potential.'[4] Such play is

> a key element in children learning to appreciate, assess and take calculated risks, which is fundamental to the development of confidence and abilities in childhood. Children seek out opportunities for risk-taking and it is the responsibility of play providers to respond with thrilling, adventurous and stimulating environments that balance risks appropriately.[5]

Herein lies the key: play needs to excite and challenge children as well as encourage them to take risks but in an environment that is essentially 'safe.' With mastery of risky elements of play comes the ability to overcome fears and anxiety. We all have to take risks in order to understand what it is to be safe.

Photograph R3 We take risks in order to understand what it is to be safe

None of us wants to put children in danger but in the twenty-first century the danger is that children are overprotected and have few opportunities to test themselves against their peers and their own capabilities and skills. Everyday living involves a high degree of risk and children need to learn how to cope with this through their play. But in over-supervising children, there is concern that adults are preventing the next generation from developing just the competence and confidence they need to become capable adults. Organized play robs children of the opportunity to innovate and learn from risk-taking behaviours.[6] Similarly, in social play children often have to pluck up courage to join others and this is a form of risk-taking. Risk and fear and the resolve to overcome that fear is a deeply personal level of play that also affects the child emotionally and intellectually: new brain research has shown that mild stress strengthens resilience by increasing the formation of new links within the brain.

Children find risky play fun – it makes them feel good. Practitioners need to provide stimulating – and, yes, risky – environments that are free from unacceptable risk but still offer children the opportunity to explore the wholeness of themselves and the wider world through their freely chosen play.

Role-play/pretend play/fantasy play

> We built a ship upon the stairs
> All made of the back-bedroom chairs,
> And filled it full of sofa pillows
> To go a-sailing on the billows.[7]

Children have always played out roles and pretended to be in worlds other than their own, as Robert Louis Stevenson so beautifully captures in this poem. Role or pretend play (together with the more extended socio-dramatic play) is claimed to be one of the highest forms of play for children because it is the forerunner and prime agent in the development of symbolic thinking. In role play children explore ways of being and becoming, and play with identities other than their own. Such play in younger children often involves domestic or other everyday scenarios, a favourite being playing 'schools' and being the adult in control. In role play children pretend to be other people or even other things, such as a pet, wild animal, monster or robot, taking them into fantasy play. There is little difference between role, pretend, fantasy play and imaginative play. In all these types of play children rearrange the world to suit their own purposes. Role, pretend and fantasy can be played alone or with others but it is more often than not (especially with children over 3-years-old) socially driven. Role and pretend play is often bound up with children's real lives.

Writing about role play, Lilian Katz[8] states:

> The benefits include not only social and emotional aspects of development but also deepening understanding of events around them: it supports their intellectual growth as they try to anticipate how things will work, what materials they will need and many other aspects of their play ... Dramatic play in which children take on roles that they become aware of from their own experiences provides satisfaction as well as opportunities to probe its multiple, complex dimensions. Many role play events provoke children to anticipate others feelings and reactions and provide real contexts for working out disagreements concerning roles and turn-taking during the play.

Pat Broadhead writes:

> One of the issues I've been thinking about is the whole business of describing play as 'role play' or 'pretend/imaginative play.' To me, this seems to diminish the play and consign it to a category of 'childishness' when, in fact, I believe children are neither in role nor pretending for much of the time, certainly not when their play materials are multi-purpose/open-ended. I think they are drawing from and reconceptualising their real life experiences ... to a much greater extent than we – as adults trying to make meaning from their play – ever give them credit for ... this is about children consciously acting out rather than 'role play'.[9]

Pat's *Social Play Continuum* is a useful tool for establishing social play dimensions.[10]

> There is a growing body of evidence supporting the many connections between cognitive competence and high-quality pretend play. If children lack opportunities to experience such play, their long-term capacities for meta-cognition, problem solving and social cognition, as well as in academic areas such as literacy, mathematics and science, may be diminished. These complex and multidimensional skills involving many areas of the brain are most likely to thrive in an atmosphere rich in high-quality pretend play.[11]

Rough and tumble

Rough and tumble (R&T) play is a form of 'fighting' play that is often enacted by parents with young babies; for example, tossing them up into the air and catching them or playing 'aeroplanes,' swinging them round and round. Toddlers like to climb on furniture and people. The most important feature of R&T play is that it is done for fun and everyone knows it is not intended to cause harm. It is also a relatively safe way to establish one's status within the group without the risk of injury that could occur during actual aggressive behaviours. Children learn a great deal about themselves, their strengths, tolerances and physical capabilities and also learn self-restraint and self-control.

The fundamental difference between real and pretend fighting is that the latter involves no intention to hurt anyone, drive them away or dominate them. Rough and tumble mimics aggressive actions and is symbolic of being aggressive but both players have to be willing partners, otherwise the play ceases. While many early years practitioners do not like the idea or physicality of R&T play, it provides children with a range of different cognitive skills. It is believed that R&T play in childhood may function as safe practice in fighting skills and as an enjoyable activity that helps to bond friendships and develop emotional control.[12]

Rough and tumble play means that children have no qualms about physical contact with each other as they engage in positive, emotional exchanges, sometimes involving tickling, or spinning each other round or playing games like leapfrog. The social signals given during R&T, such as the 'play face,' enable children to decode others' moods and feelings.[13] Rough and tumble involves substantial physical exertion and this is why (together with the safety issues) it is often not promoted by practitioners. But young children do not usually involve themselves in anything with which they do not feel safe or comfortable or which entails others in being physically aggressive: practitioners just have to negotiate a few ground rules. Like play itself, banning R&T is removing a significant play experience in children's lives that is thought to help children to avoid real fights as they establish their own and others' tolerances and strengths.

Gender differences have been found in children's R&T: boys are generally louder, more boisterous and physical than girls and tend to wrestle, chase, kick or do karate. Girls are less physical and less loud and tend to chase, spin each other round, roll about and fall on each other. Children over 5-years-old tend to be more physical than younger ones, but when older children play with younger ones they are generally less physical. Gender boundaries are crossed only for specific games; for example, chasing, where girls often encourage boys to chase them, freeze tag and wheelbarrow races, which are cross-gender.[14]

References

1. Hughes, B. (2002) *A Playworker's Taxonomy of Play Types* (2nd edn.). Ely: PlayEducation.

2. Epstein, A. (2003) How planning and reflection develop young children's thinking skills, *Beyond the Journal*. Young Children on the Web. Available online at www.journal.naeyc.org/btj/200309/Planning&Reflection.pdf (accessed 12 January 2012).

3. Sandseter, E. and Kennair, L. (2011) Children's risky play from an evolutionary perspective: the anti-phobic effects of thrilling experiences, *Evolutionary Psychology*, 9(2): 257–84.

4. Sutton-Smith, B. (1997) *The Ambiguity of Play*. Cambrige, MA: Harvard University Press (p. 89).

5. National Playing Fields Association (2000) *Best Play: What Play Provision Should do for Children*. London: National Playing Fields Association (p. 3).

6. Elkind, D. (2007) *The Power of Play Learning What Comes Naturally*. Philadelphia, PA: Da Capo Press (p. 80).

7. Stevenson, R.L. (1850–1894) In *A Child's Garden of Verses*. London: Simon & Schuster.

8. Lilian Katz (2011): personal communication.

9. Pat Broadhead (2011): personal communication.

10. Broadhead, P. (2003) *Developing Social Skills and Cooperation*. London: Routledge.

11. Bergen, D. (2002) The role of pretend play in children's cognitive development, *Early Childhood Research and Practice*, 4(1). Available online at www.ecrp.uiuc.edu/v4n1/bergen.html (accessed 23 January 2012).

12. Pelligrini, A. (2002) Rough-and-tumble play from childhood through adolescence: development and possible functions. In P.K. Smith and C. Hart (eds) *Blackwell Handbook of Social Development*. Oxford: Blackwell (pp. 438–53).

13. Carlson, F. (2009). *Rough and Tumble Play 101*. Childcare Exchange, 70–72. Available online at: www.ccie.com/resources/view_article.php?article_id= 5018870&keyword_id=120 (accessed 26 January, 2012).

14. Scott, E. and Panksepp, J. (2003) Rough-and-tumble play in human children, *Aggressive Behaviour*, 29(6): 539–51.

S

Sand play (see T = Types of play)
Schemas and play
Science and play (see C = Curriculum and play)
Self-esteem/self-image (see E = Emotional development and play)
Self-regulation (see I = Independence and self-regulation in play)
Sensory play (see M = Messy play)
Skills (see M = Mastery play)
Social development and play
Socio-dramatic play
Solitary play (see S = Social development and play)
Storying (see N = Narrative play and story)
Structured play (see Introduction)
Superhero play
Symbolic play

Schemas and play

Schemas were first researched by Piaget and refer to children's internal representation of the world: their cognitive frameworks. If new information or experiences cannot be fitted into the child's current understanding, then the child alters the existing schema or creates a whole new schema.[1] In practice, schemas have been identified by several researchers[2] as repeated patterns of behaviour that are evident in children's play and many practitioners, theorists and researchers have studied children's repeatable behaviours in line with certain categories (Table S1).

It is known that schemas change over time and, with experience, become more sophisticated. Not all children show schema development and some children have more interest in some schemas than others. Babies and young children are often driven by their schemas in play and, with maturity, show different levels of development; that is, sensory motor, symbolic, language, functional dependency (cause and effect) and abstract thought levels. Children manifest their schemas dynamically through movements and

Table S1   Types of schema[3]

Schema	Example of children's play
Transporting	Carrying objects around from one place to another (e.g. dolls in prams)
Enveloping	Covering themselves in fabric or wrapping up toys in blankets
Enclosure/containing	Filling and emptying containers, climbing into cardboard boxes, building dens
Trajectory: diagonal/ vertical/horizontal	Dropping things on floor, playing with running water, jumping off furniture, lining up cars
Rotation	Playing with wheeled toys, rolling themselves down a hill, spinning round
Connection	Joining things together (e.g. train track, or distributing and collecting toys)
Positioning	Putting things side-by-side, lying under the table
Transforming	Adding colour to dough, adding sand to the water tray

actions and configuratively in their drawings, paintings and models. It has been observed that children who have similar schemas will often play together co-operatively.

Schemas link strongly with the child's developing brain: practice, repetition and mastery make synaptic connections strong and permanent.[4]

Social development and play

Babies' first social play contacts are with their parents and, through them, babies and toddlers are gradually socialized into the wider world through this early bonding. Parent and toddler groups and nursery settings widen children's opportunities to play with others and older siblings are also part of the child's socio-cultural world. Babies learn social nuances playfully from facial expressions, movements, verbal interactions and body language: experts believe that the first year of a child's life is crucial as a secure basis for future cognitive, social and emotional development and competence in language.[5]

When children play with others they are learning to deal with the complexities of life and relationships: knocking over someone else's model because they would not pass you the scissors is decidedly antisocial! But through their actions and others' reactions most children learn the social skills required to 'play nicely.' 'Children need a combination of intellectual skills, motivational qualities, and socio-emotional skills to succeed in school.'[6] Research investigating the involvement of adults in children's play found that 'the significance of play for the social interplay ... is that it is fun, children and adults appreciate and learn from each other, and it is a way to be together and get insight into how the other thinks in play.'[7]

Photograph S1 Children's collaborative social play

Children's overall success in making friends and settling into new situations is dependent on their maturity in social development and their ability to play co-operatively.

> ... young children [must] be able to: understand their own feelings and the viewpoints and feelings of others, cooperate with both peers and adults, resolve conflict successfully and control their own behavior. Evidence shows that young children who have established positive relationships with parents, caregivers and teachers are secure and confident in exploring new situations and mastering learning challenges.[8]

Social and emotional development has strong links.

It is known that play is vital to children's social development and that 'play activities are socially and symbolically complex and involve social reciprocity which is the core of affective and personality development.'[9] Play enables children to:

- practise communication and negotiation skills and appreciate the feelings of others;
- respond to their peers' and siblings' feelings, waiting for a turn and sharing;
- experiment with roles through pretend and socio-dramatic play;
- experience others' points of view, work through conflicts and understand rules in play.[10]

Social play also involves a range of other learning features such as conformity, response to peer pressure, obedience, leadership, persuasion, compliance, personal identification, status and reciprocity.

Socio-dramatic play

Socio-dramatic play is similar to role/pretend play but is different in that the play is always shared and sustained (10 minutes or more) and usually has a verbalized ongoing theme or story.[11] Socio-dramatic play usually involves the enactment of real and potential experiences of an intense personal, social, domestic or interpersonal nature and involves plots, props and roles. For example, playing at house, going to the shops, being mothers and fathers, organizing a meal or even having an argument are typical contexts for socio-dramatic play among younger children. As children mature, the play may become more associated with media characters (e.g. see S = Superhero play) or be related to fantasy situations like monsters and dragons.

Boys and girls differ in their socio-dramatic play, with boys often playing out stories relating to police or fire officers, monsters or kung-fu fighters with good and bad guys. Girls engage in socio-dramatic play more than boys and their play frequently involves houses, families and talent shows and is often collaborative and about relationships.[12] But all children use socio-dramatic play to assume features of the adult world in order to instigate innovative play routines in their peer cultures: their playful narratives are creative and fun.[13]

Socio-dramatic play is influential in developing children's self-regulation, as children are highly motivated to stick to roles and rules within the play and acquire the ability to inhibit their impulses, act in co-ordination with others and generate plans and strategies. High-level dramatic play has been shown to have significant cognitive, social and emotional benefits. In research, the relationship between socio-dramatic play and gains in self-regulation was especially strong for highly impulsive preschoolers.[14] Other major research about socio-dramatic play has shown that:

... children's language turned out to be significantly more advanced and 'literate' with more syntactically complete and complicated utterances, use of explicit references and elaborated nominal groups in socio-dramatic play than in any other play activity ... The demands of conveying meaning to peers in dramatic play contexts seem to provide children with opportunities to practise 'literate' language, language that is similar to what is demanded when writing for an absent audience.[15]

Example S1

Three boys in the nursery are discussing aeroplanes and how they had flown to the seaside for their holidays. They decide to make an aeroplane in the classroom and proceed to gather chairs for seats, tubes (from water play) for the oxygen masks, and cushions from the reading area for the life-jackets. They then gather two other children and all get themselves 'seated.' One boy jumps up to find something to use as safety straps but tells the others 'You'll just have to pretend' when he can not find anything suitable. There is a short 'argument' while another boy finds rope but is told it is not suitable. The practitioner, who is observing but not interacting, is very surprised when she hears one of the children using a deep adult voice announce: 'Ladies and gentleman ... welcome on board. Please make yourselves comfortable and please don't smoke!'

This socio-dramatic play lasted for over an hour and in that time individual children showed a wide range of social and cognitive skills, some of which were a great surprise to the practitioner, particularly the child making the announcement who was not known for his confidence. As the boys' play unfolds, they are engaged, concentrating and collaborating, and showing focused thinking and self-control. As they sort out passengers and crew, they are taking the perspectives of those people. In the use of resources, they are exhibiting and creating symbolic representations and making connections and evaluating and thinking critically about the next stage in their play. Their narratives are clear and complex.

Superhero play

Superhero play has received a great deal of attention from parents and educators in the recent past, some practitioners believing that superhero play increases the levels of noise and aggression in classrooms. Superheroes are often characters from television or electronic games and can often appear to be violent. Practitioners have real concerns for the safety of children and worries about whether children – boys in particular – will learn to be violent rather than learn to control such negative emotions.[16] However, no such evidence exists and, in fact, children playing out such roles are learning to cope with the ups and downs of life.[17]

With guns, adults know that they can be banned but also that children will still take the opportunity to turn anything into a gun or sword – even a banana (representational and symbolic play). Far from banning guns and swords in superhero and other forms of role play, such play appears to have an important developmental function in young children although not all children engage in superhero or violent/war play.

Children playing at superheroes are often working out how to cope with the violence they see, perhaps in their homes and communities and certainly on television: war is a regular feature of television news and playing 'soldiers' (especially if your mum or dad is one) helps a child to understand others' roles and responsibilities. Being a superhero can help children focus on those things that frighten or scare them and in their play they can struggle to work it out and understand their own feelings. Superhero play also enables children to feel something they rarely do: powerful and strong, sometimes even invincible, like cartoon and computer game characters. Children engaged in superhero play are often 'working on social, moral and intellectual issues in positive ways.'[18] Children also gain affiliation to their peer group and a sense of inclusion, as they co-operate, negotiate and sometimes lead the play. Watching the same superheroes on television enables young children to share cultural experiences with others. Superhero play can also be a great outlet for energy and a wonderful stimulus for the imagination.[19]

Practitioners should make time to observe the play and learn to understand what superhero and war play means to the children involved: what they experience, why and how. This information can then be used not only to reflect on this type of play for their own understanding but to help children think about the underlying violent content of their play and deal with it.[20] Providing props, costumes and play spaces helps development of all role play.

Symbolic play

Symbolic play emerges during a child's second year and its appearance demonstrates that the child can substitute one thing for another, holding on to a mental picture and recreating it in the mind. Symbolic play develops in ever-increasing complexity as children mature and is linked closely with emotion, cognition, problem solving, creativity and well-being: it is considered to be one of the most significant developments in the young child, connected strongly with future success in school. It is also an important scaffold to emerging language and literacy because children can begin to think in the abstract and, therefore, relate, for example, pictures to objects and numbers and letters to symbols.[21]

References

1. Piaget, J. (1980) *Adaptation and Intelligence*. Chicago, IL: University of Chicago Press.
2. Arnold, C. (2010) *Understanding Schemas and Emotion in Early Childhood*. London: Sage Publications. See also Athey, C. (2007) *Extending Thought in Young Children: A Parent–Teacher Partnership* (2nd edn.). London: Sage Publications.
3. Adapted from Louis, S., Beswick, C., McGraw, L., Hayes, L. and Featherstone, S. (2008) *Again! Again! Understanding Schemas in Young Children*. London: A&C Black.
4. Meade, A. and Cubey, P. (2008) *Thinking Children: Learning about Schemas*. Maidenhead: Open University Press.
5. Raikes, H. (1996) A secure base for babies: applying attachment concepts to the infant care setting, *Young Children*, 51(5): 59–67 (p. 59).
6. Thompson, R. (2001) The roots of school readiness in social and emotional development. Set for success: building a strong foundation for school readiness based on the social-emotional development of young children, *Kauffman Early Education Exchange*, 1(1): 8–29. Kansas City, MO: The Ewing Marion Kauffman Foundation. Available online at www.sites.kauffman.org/pdf/eex_brochure.pdf (accessed 24 January 2012).
7. Vickerius, M. and Sandberg, A. (2006) The significance of play and the environment around play, *Early Child Development and Care*, 176(2): 207–17 (p. 211).
8. Klein, L. (2002) *Set for Success: Building A Strong Foundation for School Readiness Based on the Social-emotional Development of Young Children*. Ewing Marion Kauffman Foundation. Available online at www.childcareresearch.org/childcare/resources/13495?publisher=Ewing+Marion+Kauffman+Foundation (accessed 24 January 2012).
9. DeVries, R. (1997) Piaget's social theory, *Educational Researcher*, 26(2): 4–17.
10. Adapted from Isenberg, J. and Jalongo, M. (2006) *Creative Thinking and Arts-based Learning: Preschool Through Fourth Grade*. Boston, MA: Pearson Allyn Bacon Prentice Hall (pp. 53–55).
11. Smilansky, S. and Shefatya, L. (1990) *Facilitating Play: A Medium for Promoting Cognitive, Socio-emotional, and Academic Development in Young Children*. Gaithersburg, MD: Psychological and Educational Publications.

12. Martin, B. (2011) *Children at Play: Learning Gender in the Early Years*. Stoke-on-Trent: Trentham Books (Ch. 5).
13. Corsaro, W. (2003) *We're Friends, Right?: Inside Kids' Culture*. Washington, DC: Joseph Henry Press.
14. Elias, C. and Berk, L. (2002) Self-regulation in young children: is there a role for sociodramatic play? *Early Childhood Research Quarterly*, 17: 1–17.
15. Vedeler, L. (1997) Dramatic play: a format for 'literate' language? *British Journal of Educational Psychology*, 67(2): 153–67.
16. Holland, P. (2003) *'We Don't Play With Guns Here': War, Weapon and Superhero Play in the Early Years*. Maidenhead: Open University Press
17. Katch, J. (2001) *Under Deadman's Skin: Discovering the Meaning of Children's Violent Play*. Boston, MA: Beacon.
18. Levin, D. (2006) Play with violence: understanding and responding effectively. In D. Fromberg and D. Bergin (eds) *Play from Birth to Twelve: Contexts, Perspectives, and Meanings* (2nd edn.). New York and Abingdon: Taylor & Francis Group (p. 397).
19. Paley, V.G. (1986) *Boys and Girls: Superheroes in the Doll Corner*. Chicago and London: Chicago University Press.
20. Adams, S. and Moyles, J. (2005) *Images of Violence: Responding to Children's Representations of the Violence They See*. London: Featherstone Educational/A&C Black.
21. Worthington, M. (2010) Play is a complex landscape: imagination and symbolic meanings. In P. Broadhead, L. Wood and J. Howard (eds) *Play and Learning in Educational Settings*. London: Sage Publications.

T

Technology and play

Technology and play includes a vast range of different electronic toys and other technological media; for example, television, cameras, Wii, Play Stations. Current research into this area is equally vast but the jury tends to be out in relation to whether electronic forms of play are good or bad for young children. Some play researchers feel that electronic toys take away any opportunity children might have for wondering and understanding how things 'work'[1] whereas others feel that children gain different kinds of skills and understandings from using current technologies.[2] Whatever we all think, the technology is here to stay, advancing daily, and children seem to love it! Today's children are immersed in an enveloping culture of media that is impossible for them to ignore. Young children actually spend more time than older ones in front of screens than older children who are immersed in games and sports as leisure play.[3]

A major concern among many educators is that children spend too much time indoors and there is a cultural loss in relation to childhood play and games as well as significant issues related to health and obesity.[4] Many young children are thought to spend between three and four hours watching television daily, with benefits being to entertain, to inform, to enter fantasy worlds and for quiet, solitary play. But with young children and play the concerns are cognitively related: when children sort items such as real food with an adult they are experiencing the three-dimensional object, physically handling it with all their senses. When, however, a sorting game such as this is played on the computer there is no touch, smell or feel element, which means that children are missing out on something essential to their understanding.[5] 'Young children need a real rather than a virtual reality.'[6] Smith suggests that computer play is only one type of play – games play – because computer games automatically have built-in rules.[7]

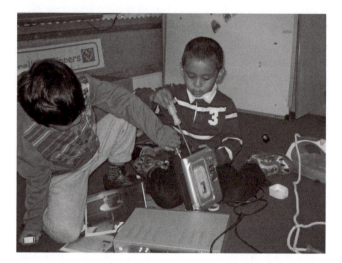

Photograph T1 Finding out how things work for real

Yet, increasingly many young children's lives are dominated by the virtual world as is evidenced by the length of time that even very young children now spend in front of 'screen technology.'[8] The effect on children's play can be significant; for example, where their imaginative role play often centres around imitations of shows, such as 'X Factor' or 'Big Brother,' which can actually limit children's play (in trying to imitate) rather than enhance and extend it. Exposure to screen technologies has been associated with greater attention problems throughout childhood[9] and it is common to hear practitioners say children just do not listen (or play) like they used to. Communication is two-way and there is little verbal interaction with a television screen and limited verbal interaction with most computer games.

The main requirement for young children is that the media and digital toys should generate play and social interactions. Children's play with some media such as cameras can really enhance opportunities not only for learning to use and understand the media but also for capturing their own and other children's play experiences and reflecting on them. Using computers gives children certain co-ordination skills but nothing can replace real hands-on play experiences – like stringing beads, manipulating dough, using scissors and glue, handling different toys – for the development of co-ordination and manual dexterity. Children need these skills in order to hold pencils and crayons and eventually to shape letters and numbers. They need these skills even for punching in letters on mobile phones!

Another effect of media dominance is that older children now spend more time with children of their own age rather than in cross-age cultural play and games from which the younger children were known to learn new skills and knowledge.

Therapeutic (cathartic) play

Therapeutic play (cathartic play) helps children to come to terms with events in their lives that they find painful or emotionally challenging: children play out within their role and dramatic play scenarios things that they do not understand so that they can gain some control over their lives. Through play, children also create their own self-protection from anxieties and enhance their adaptive capabilities and resilience.

Example T1

A new baby has been born in Martha's family and she does not like it much! It takes up a lot of the time that mummy used to play with her – now she is bathing the baby, smiling at it, tickling it and Martha is, yes, jealous! Whenever she gets the opportunity, she hides something of the baby's or pokes his tummy as she goes by. Mummy says the baby will play with her when he is older but how long will that be? In the nursery, Martha has increasingly taken to playing in the home area with the baby dolls. She and her friend Edie (both of them 3-years-old) constantly bath and change the baby together, then push it around the nursery in the pushchair. Sometimes Martha plays 'baby' to Edie's mummy and sometimes they reverse those roles. The practitioner decides to ask Martha and other children to bring in photographs of themselves as babies and takes the opportunity to talk with the children about what it must feel like to be a helpless baby and how useful it is to have an older brother or sister to feed you, play with you and help look after you.

This gentle therapy worked with Martha and she was able to play out her feelings and discuss them with a sensitive adult and with other children, who also took the chance to talk about new babies in their homes. Martha's mum was encouraged to bring the baby into school, which gave Martha some 'kudos' on the baby front!

Sensitive practitioners are often alerted by changes in the child's play behaviours to challenges the child is experiencing. Children who have previously been altruistic and forthcoming but suddenly withdraw into themselves are usually expressing a problem that needs to be investigated. It could just be the new baby at home or friendship concerns but could go deeper. With some children, especially those who have suffered abuse – and this often shows in the destructive and highly emotional nature of their play – psychologically based therapies are needed which, with young children, are always based on play and what observers can learn from the ways in which children play and their verbalizations of that play. In this way, they can explore playful ways to re-establish the child's security, self-concept and confidence and their mastery of the situation and their emotions.[10]

All forms of play therapy are conducted in safe environments, the therapy being based on understanding how children play and how, through their play, they express wishes, fantasies, internal conflicts and perceptions of their world. Counsellors often encourage children to bring a favourite toy to play therapy sessions, to draw pictures, use puppets or act out fantasies with toys such as small worlds people. Once the psychotherapist has drawn out the child's problem, then play is used to help children deal with the situation.

Transformational play

Transformational play is sometimes called 'deep play,' which is creative and seeks to construct new ways of 'being' in the world. In play children can transform themselves or the objects they are using (symbolic or representational play). Creative people are often transformational in their approach to the world, seeking to transform what they see, hear or experience into something completely different, like impressionist painters or music composers. In children, transformational play is linked to role play and socio-dramatic play but also to novel ways of using play materials. Play by its multimodal, open-ended nature expands the manner in which we deal with concepts and ideas, leading to transformational ways of thinking and opening new doors through unexpected breakthroughs:[11] in other words, it is the stuff of invention and innovating thinking. Inventors and artists, together with mathematicians and scientists, play with distinctions and boundaries, truths and the limits of knowledge and, through play, transform ideas.

Transformational play transcends the reality of life in order to germinate new ideas, and shape and reshape them. Children's transformational play is often exhibited in making up role-play stories (sometimes media-based inventions) but taking them to the limits of how they might be played.

> **Example T2**
>
> Rupal, Najir and Kazim (6-years-old) are deep in the forest looking for a place to hide from the 'searchers.' They are aware of other children close behind them and decide to climb one of the trees. They discover a whole canopy that hides them from intending pursuers. But they also discover another world where there are all sorts of imaginary creatures, monsters, dragons and frightening things. They 'brave' this world until all below them has moved on – and they have not been found! They are ecstatic at having eluded the searchers and in a kind of awe and euphoria about the world they have 'discovered.'

While this example of deep play is at the level of three young children, older children take deep play to riskier extremes, such as playing 'chicken' in crossing the road, climbing to extreme heights and driving bikes at erratic and dangerous speeds.[12]

Any aspect of play can be 'transformed' – in other words, made significantly deeper and more thoughtful – and engage children with their meta-cognitive awareness. In real and fantasy play, children gradually come to realize the connections with the real world and transform their thinking.[13]

Types of play

Types of play covers a multitude of different aspects of play including many already discussed in other sections, such as:

- rough and tumble;
- socio-dramatic play;
- social play;
- creative play;
- communication play;
- role play;
- symbolic play;
- deep play;
- exploratory play;
- fantasy/imaginative play;

- locomotor play;
- mastery play;
- object play;
- recapitulative play.

Types of play also includes the provision of play areas or stations by practitioners in consultation with children, which are identified in Table T1.

All these areas should reflect the cultural and ethnic diversity of the children to ensure inclusion for those children with individual needs as well as appealing to both boys and girls. For babies and young children, the addition of soft play and sleeping areas need to be considered. None of these areas

Table T1 Areas for play

Home/domestic area	e.g. kitchen, bed, table and chairs, telephone, calculator, shopping list and pencils, dressing up, kitchen equipment
Constructional area	e.g. wooden blocks, linking bricks, cardboard boxes
Outdoor area	e.g. for experiencing the natural world, including seed growing, sensory garden
Miniature worlds area	e.g. road layout mats, small figures, vehicles, houses, animals
Natural materials area	e.g. conkers, nuts, leaves, twigs, a wormery, shells, stones, driftwood, rock
Manipulative area	e.g. woodwork, musical instruments
Messy area	e.g. sand, water, paints, cornflour and water, shaving foam, gloop, ice, sawdust
'Whatever you want it to be' area[14]	e.g. cardboard boxes, fabrics, tubes
Media area	e.g. cameras, computers, laptops, CD player, recorder, microphone
Quiet area	e.g. dens or covered spaces where children can hide and be calm and quiet, soft toys, bean bag seats
Locomotor play, including opportunities for rough and tumble, boisterous play	e.g. climbing frames, bats/balls, hoops and other physical play equipment
Role play/pretend/fantasy/imaginative/ socio-dramatic area	e.g. shop, hairdressers, café, aeroplane, bus, capes
Exploratory/discovery/investigative area,	e.g. old clocks, radios, telephones to take apart, treasure baskets, magnets, magnifying glasses
Creative play area	e.g. clay, paints, glue, marking-making resources, found materials, crayons, chalks, felt-tip pens

should be considered to be discrete: in their self-chosen play activities, children may select to take water to the sand tray or use bricks in the home corner to develop different resources. They may choose to take their role play outdoors. It will not be possible in some settings to provide all these areas all the time; for example, the home area may have to double up as the role-play areas as a garage, shop or hairdressers, and creative and messy areas may also have to be located together. Similarly, computers and other technological media may be distributed to other areas; for example, a laptop in the role play or home areas.

In addition, children may choose to play alone (solitary), watch others play (onlooker), play alongside others and mimic their play (parallel), play in a semi-co-operative way with others doing similar things (associative play), engage in a pair or group play situation (co-operative), engage fully in a deeper play situation with others, carrying out storying or other involved play scenarios (collaborative) or play games with others (competitive).

The good practitioners will monitor the areas, individual children's use of them, the quality of the materials and resulting play experiences in an endeavour to check that all children are getting the widest range of experiences possible over the course of half a term or more.

References

1. Elkind, D. (2007) (op. cit.: p. 23).
2. Courage, M. and Setliff, A. (2009) Debating the impact of television and video material on very young children: attention, learning, and the developing brain, *Society for Research in Child Development*, 3(1): 72–78.
3. Wartella, E., Lee, J. and Caplovitz, A. (2002) *Children and Interactive Media: Research Compendium Update*. Austin, TX: University of Texas.
4. Davies, M. (2010) *Children, Media and Culture*. Maidenhead: Open University Press.
5. Healy, J. (1999) *Failure to Connect: How Computers Affect Our Children's Minds*. New York: Simon & Schuster/Touchstone.
6. Oldfield, L. (2011) The Steiner Waldorf Foundation Stage – 'To everything there is a season'. In R. House (ed.) *Too Much, Too Soon? Early Learning and the Erosion of Childhood*. Stroud: Hawthorne Press (p. 187).
7. Smith, P.K. (2010) *Children and Play*. Oxford: Wiley/Blackwell (p. 12).
8. Sigman, A. (2007) *Remotely Controlled: How Television is Damaging our Lives*. London: Vermillion.
9. Swing, E., Gentile, D., Anderson, C. and Walsh, D. (2010) Television and video game exposure and the development of attention problems, *Pediatrics*, 126(2): 214–21.
10. Schaefer, C., Kelly-Zion, S., McCormick, J. and Ohnogi, A. (2008) *Play Therapy for Very Young Children*. Lanham, MD: Jason Aronson/Rowman and Littlefield.

11. See website www.msuedtechsandbox.com/MAETVAULT/category-descrip tions/7-cognitive-tools/deep-play-transformational-play/ (accessed 27 January 2012).

12. Sutton-Smith, B. and Kelly-Byrne, D. (1984) The idealization of play. In P.K. Smith (ed.) *Play in Animals and Humans*. Oxford: Basil Blackwell (pp. 305–21).

13. Roopnarine, J.L., Shin, M., Jung, K. and Hossain, Z. (2003) Play and early development and education: the instantiation of parental belief systems. In O. Saracho and B. Spodek (eds) *Contemporary Issues in Early Childhood Education*. Greenwich, CT: New Age Publishers.

14. Broadhead, P. and Burt, A. (2011) *Understanding Young Children's Learning Through Play: Building Playful Pedagogies*. London: Routledge.

U

Understanding (see C = Cognitive play and learning and metacognition)
United Nations Convention on the Rights of the Child – right to play
Universality of play
Unstructured play (see Introduction)

United Nations Convention on the Rights of the Child – right to play

Childhood is not a time to prepare children for adulthood but a period of life in its own right. During this childhood period, children have the right to play for all the reasons outlined in previous pages. Children's right to play is enshrined in the *United Nations Convention on the Rights of the Child* (UNCRC) (1989), Article 31:

> 1. State Parties recognize the right of the child to rest and leisure, to engage in play and recreational activities appropriate to the age of the child and to participate freely in cultural life and the arts.
> 2. State Parties shall respect and promote the right of the child to participate fully in cultural and artistic life and shall encourage the provision of appropriate and equal opportunities for cultural, artistic, recreational and leisure activity.
>
> (N.B. 'State Parties' means all those countries who uphold the contents of the Convention.)

The UNCRC appears to acknowledge that 'Play is not a luxury to be considered after other rights; it is an essential and integral component underpinning the four principles of the UNCRC – non-discrimination, survival and development, the best interests of the child and participation.'[1]

Acknowledging children's right to play means that adults must recognize, respect and promote the importance of play in children's lives. This means practitioners making effective provision for play, protecting children's right to play by understanding and valuing play and conveying this value to others including parents, and participating in children's play on children's own terms. 'Children, as children, have a different, or "other", way of seeing, feeling and acting in the world, which comes alive in their play.'[2] Practitioners can support children's right to play by reviewing the setting or school from the perspective of the children – how far are children allowed agency and ownership in their activities? How is this expressed to them? Do a few children dominate play provision or is it inclusive of all? When children are deeply involved in play scenarios, is their right to play respected or do adults intervene with requests that children 'do some work' or 'play somewhere else?'

Reggio Emilia is an example of a play-based curricular process that emphasizes the importance of children's rights and dignity and the adults' responsibilities to listen to children's voices.[3] This is consistent with a recent literature review that states:

> If play is understood as not controlled by adults, as interwoven into the fabric of daily life, then there is a need to think beyond providing adult-sanctioned, dedicated places and programmes for play. Instead, we must move towards a broader ecological, political, economic and cross-cutting consideration of children's ability to realise their right to play in their daily lives and in their local neighbourhoods, thereby retaining that control.[4]

Photograph U1 Every child has the right to play

Universality of play

The urge to play is universal in children (and in adults!). It is also a historical phenomenon, evidence of which has been found in many different societies over thousands of years, attesting to its universality in different cultures and societies. 'Although human societies vary in the amount and type of such play, anthropological accounts attest that fully developed pretend play... appears to be universal.'[5] Perhaps this play is functional in that it enables people past and present to try out different roles, understand others' perspectives and gain survival skills.

Universality of play applies to animals as well as humans: it is known that all higher animals behave very playfully as infants and much of their play is similar to young children, for example, rough and tumble episodes in ape communities and toy play in cats and dogs. The universality of play is strong evidence that it has value across place and time to adults and children: otherwise it would not endure in this way and offer humans an evolutionary advantage. All children follow much the same developmental pattern wherever they live in the world: this suggests that children's development is based upon a biologically predetermined progression in both play and maturity that is vital. Neither childhood nor play should be rushed: the role of immaturity is to ensure that children's special ways of learning and knowing, qualitatively different from those of adults, will enable them to gain a unique foundation upon which later innovations, creativity and knowledge will emerge.[6] After all, adult behaviours are always a result of just those developmental, playful stages that the child experienced.

Elizabeth Brooker, who has studied children's play extensively, writes:

- Young children's play is universally recognised by families as important for their well-being and development;
- In traditional societies, play is viewed simply as a pastime for children, or a preparation for growing up, whereas in many western societies it is seen as the means for children to begin their school learning.

Nevertheless, the apparently universal appreciation of 'pretend play' as a preparation for adult life, and a space to try out cultural behaviours, suggests that parents everywhere are able to identify a role for play in preparing children for participation in the community, if not for teaching them school-like knowledge and skills.[7]

References

1. Lester, S. and Russell, W. (2010) *Children's Right to Play: An Examination of the Importance of Play in the Lives of Children*. The Hague: Bernard Van Leer Foundation (p. x).

2. Lester, S. and Russell, W. (ibid.) (p. 7).
3. Hall, E. and Rudkin, J. (2010) *Seen and Heard: Children's Rights in Early Childhood Education*. NAEYC publication, New York: Teachers' College Press.
4. Lester, S. and Russell, W. (op. cit.: p. 2).
5. Bornstein, M. (2006) On the significance of social relationships in the development of children's earliest symbolic play: an ecological perspective. In A. Göncü and S. Gaskins (eds) *Play and Development: Evolutionary, Sociocultural and Functional perspectives*. Mahwaw, NJ: Lawrence Erlbaum Associates (p. 115).
6. Bjorkland, D. (2007) *Why Youth is Not Wasted on the Young*. Malden, MA: Blackwell.
7. Elizabeth Brooker (2011): personal communication.

Values in play and playfulness

> Each second we live is a new and unique moment of the universe, a moment that will never be again. And what do we teach our children? We teach them that two and two make four, and that Paris is the capital of France. When will we also teach them what they are? We should say to each of them: Do you know what you are? You are a marvel. You are unique. In all the years that have passed, there has never been another child like you. Your legs, your arms, your clever fingers, the way you move. You may become a Shakespeare, a Michelangelo, a Beethoven. You have the capacity for anything. Yes, you are a marvel ... You must work – we must all work – to make the world worthy of its children.[1]
>
> (Picasso 1881–1973)

Unlike Picasso who, in this excerpt, shows his value of children, their play and learning and the relationship with creativity, many adults see play and learning as opposites and try to separate out these two processes. Yet all of us have played as children and, as adults, continue to do so without necessarily recognizing it. Analysing his love of mountain biking against play values, the blogger in Example V1 wrote:

Example V1

For me, mountain biking has two distinct states.1) At times as I sweep down trails at speed, it affords me the ability to clear my mind of all conscious, verbal thought – at these times I am 'in the moment,' riding and reacting to the tasks at hand, not thinking of anything. These are the most 'fun' moments in mountain biking where the means are more valued than the ends and involve an active, alert but non-stressed frame of mind ... 2) At other times, I fall into a pedalling rhythm and my mind is free to wander on to subjects often completely unrelated to riding. These thoughts often touch on issues I'm facing in my real life (e.g. work, my children), affording me pressure-free environment for free association on such topics ... I would say that sometimes on my bike I am playing – that is when I'm really attuned to the biking, to going faster, etc. In doing so I might even imagine that I'm in the Tour de France. Other times I'm just cruising along enjoying the wind, view, rhythmic activity and my own free-floating thoughts.

The value of play to this adult is clear and is little different from what we understand about the value to children of play and playfulness.

Dorothy Selleck[2] tells a wonderful story about Theodore, aged 2 (Example V2).

Theodore would turn himself into a roaring lion at times ... whether to assert himself in his older brother's games or even when a wasp hovered near his ice-cream! His roars helped him feel twice the size and enabled him to be accepted into the dens and 'derring-do' of the older children. Sadly, his roaring omnipotence did not deter the wasp – much to his astonishment! Play at lions was his way of saying *'Can I join in'* ... or *'Go away,'* or *'I want you to come this way with me,'* or ... something else! We can never be certain of a child's meaning, or the value they attach to the play, but the more we watch and wonder and take time to be uncertain about the possibilities that could be in the child's heart and mind, the more meaningful our interjections and responses are likely to be.

The value of either of these is apparent in the observations – and play's value goes still further. One longitudinal study found that children in play-ful learning or child-initiated learning environments showed superior social

behaviours, fewer conduct disorders, enhanced academic performance and re-
tention beyond children who experienced didactic instruction and play learning.[3] Another study has concluded that: '... play is a force that enables us to
discover our most essential selves, to find fulfillment and growth.' By studying murderers in Texas prisons, the same researcher found that the absence
of play in childhood is an important predictor of criminality and concludes
that play is vital to our mental health and well-being throughout our lives.[4]

Practitioners need to emphazise to children and adults the value of play
in their own lives if either are to recognize children's development through
play. The value of play and playfulness lies in appreciating the variety of
human play experiences and play cultures within childhood and throughout
our lives.

Voice – children's voices in play

Giving children a voice is closely related to children's rights and to power
relations between children and adults. Children have the right to have their
voices heard in matters that affect them deeply such as play and learning experiences. While for long it has been felt that young children will not
understand enough to contribute to decisions about their play and lives
in general, much research working with children has shown that, with
appropriate support,

> Every child, whatever their age or ability, is capable of self-expression.
> Children's imaginations, ideas, opinions, feelings, needs and worries
> can be expressed in so many different ways – through words for those
> able to talk or sign, as well as physical movements and body language,
> non-verbal sounds, or creative expression like play, dance, music and
> art. The people in charge of reforming children's services must em-
> brace the clear message that children's voices must be heard, listened
> to and understood.[5]

Honouring children's voices in our dealings with them in their play is
a necessarily democratic process[6] that comes with responsibilities. 'Whilst
not all of what children want will be consistent or achievable, once their
views are sought adults have a responsibility to respond to them ethically
and with respect.'[7] Justifications for giving voice to children can be made
from an educational as well as a sociological point of view.[8] In one study of
3–4-year-olds, the researchers found that:

> young children do have a voice and that what they have to tell us
> is interesting and informative ... For many years early years experts

have been arguing that young children require a constructivist, play-based curriculum ... The findings from this study would support this curricular approach, where it would appear that it is in tune with the thinking of three-four year old children.[9]

Children in this study wanted to be actively engaged in the learning process through exploration in favoured play situations where they could use their own initiative, imagination and physicality. They did not want to sit for long periods of time; girls valued the home corner best and boys the construction area and sand tray. Children enjoyed using the camera as a physical tool to express their opinions. '... children emphasised the desire to be creative and imaginative in their learning, choosing activities which allowed them to transform into another role, or engage in the process of creating something of importance to themselves.'[10]

Photograph V1 Children's voices and choices

It is evident from this and other research that practitioners have a clear responsibility to hear children's voices and ensure children's views and opinions on the play and learning opportunities they experience in early years classrooms and settings are acknowledged, respected and incorporated.

References

1. Available online at www.thinkexist.com/quotation/each_second_we_live_is_a_new_and_unique_moment_of/339726.html (accessed 13 March 2012).
2. Dorothy Selleck (2012): personal communication.

3. Marcon, R. (2002) Moving up the grades: relationship between preschool model and later school success, *Early Childhood Research and Practice*, 4(1). Available online at www.ecrp.uiuc.edu/v4n1/marcon.html (accessed 3 February 2012).

4. Brown, S. and Vaughan, C. (2010) *Play: How it Shapes the Brain, Opens the Imagination, and Invigorates the Soul*. New York: Tarcher/Penguin Putnam (p. 25).

5. Bob Reitemeier (2011) 'We must listen to children', reported in *The Guardian*, 12 May. Available online at www.guardian.co.uk/society/joepublic/2011/may/12/bob-reitemeier-munro-report-listen-to-the-children (accessed 31 January 2012).

6. Clark, A. and Moss, P. (2001) *Listening to Young Children: The Mosaic Approach*. London: National Children's Bureau for the Joseph Rowntree Foundation.

7. MacNaughton, G., Smith, K. and Lawrence, H. (2002) *Consulting with Children Birth to Eight Years of Age: Hearing Young Children's Voices*. Australia: Centre for Equity and Innovation in Early Childhood. Available online at www.children.act.gov.au/documents/PDF/under5report.pdf (accessed 2 February 2012) (p. 75).

8. Lloyd-Smith, M. and Tarr, J. (2000) Researching children's perspectives: a sociological dimension. In A. Lewis and G. Lindsay (eds) *Researching Children's Perspectives*. Maidenhead: Open University Press.

9. Cunningham, J., Walsh, G., Dunn, J., Mitchell, D. and McAlister, M. (2004) *Giving Children a Voice: Accessing the Views and Interests of Three-Four Year Old Children in Playgroup*. Belfast: DHSSPS (pp. 89, 91).

10. Cunningham et al. (ibid.) (p. 92).

W

Wii play

The Wii (and other movement/gesture systems) feature digital sensors that let children (and adults) play a game virtually rather than for real. However, the exercise undertaken in the use of the Wii is very real, whether it is obstacle courses, riding a Segway or a bike or running round a virtual environment popping balloons, and most seem to find it fun! It can be undertaken in the safety of children's own homes rather than being outside. Games can be played alone or in competition with others but also through teamwork. These games are known to encourage exercise: energy expenditure more than doubles when sedentary screen time is converted to active screen time according to recent research.[1] But games selection needs care if adults are trying to avoid aggression in the children's games as even some innocuous looking Wii games are quite violent.

It is worth remembering, though, that even these active games are no substitute for real outdoor play and the multi-sensory experience that this provides. And, of course, the younger the child the less time they should spend in screen-based activities.[2] Wii is thought to encourage families to play together but, again, this screen-based time has been shown sometimes to be at the expense of reading or just talking together.[3]

Too much time spent on games such as those on Wii and other screen-based technologies are thought to contribute to sleep problems, stress and vision problems in children. It is recommended that children under

Ludic play

Ludic play has already been introduced in epistemic play where it was described as one of the three elements of Hutt's play typology. Ludic means 'play' and is usually associated with showing spontaneous and undirected playfulness. Ludic play refers to children's imaginative, fantasy and sociodramatic play – that is, 'what if' scenarios or pretence – and is often associated with fun and freedom.

Ludic can also refer to creativity;[12] playing with ideas and thoughts to explore possibilities.

References

1. Dunn, J. (1993) *Young Children's Close Relationships: Beyond Attachment.* Newbury, CA: Sage Publications.
2. Cook, G. (2000) *Language Play, Language Learning.* New York and Oxford: Oxford University Press.
3. Garvey, C. (1990) *Play.* Cambridge, MA: Harvard University Press.
4. Garcia, O. cited in Leong, C. (2009) *Play Develops Language Skills.* Available online at www.4children.org/files/articles/424/709ecee.pdf (accessed 18 January 2012).
5. Stone, S. and Stone, W. (undated) *Symbolic Play and Emergent Literacy.* Available online at www.iccp-play.org/documents/brno/stone1.pdf (accessed 25 January 2012).
6. Lewis, P., Boucher, J. Lupton, L. and Watson, S. (2000) Relationships between symbolic play, functional play, verbal and non-verbal ability in young children, *International Journal of Language and Communication Disorders*, 35(1): 117–27.
7. Marian Whitehead (2012): personal communication.
8. Clark, A. and Moss, P. (2008) *Spaces to Play: More Listening to Young Children Using the Mosaic Approach.* London: National Children's Bureau.
9. Palmer S. (2006) *Talk to Me! Early Years Practitioners and Parents Working Together to Develop Children's Speaking and Listening Skills.* London: Basic Skills Agency.
10. Bayley, R. and Broadbent, L. (2001) *Helping Young Children to Listen.* Birmingham: Lawrence Educational Publishers.
11. Evans, R. and Jones, D. (eds) *Metacognitive Approaches to Developing Oracy: Developing Speaking and Listening with Young Children.* London: Routledge.
12. Compton, A., Johnson, J., Nahmad-Williams, L. and Taylor, K. (2010) *Creative Development.* London: Continuum.

Photograph W1   Three-year-old playing on the Wii

3-years-old should not engage in screen-based activities at all and that those aged between 3 and 7 should watch no more than 30 minutes to an hour of television a day. This is because while computer games may be more stimulating than watching television or DVDs, 'even this so-called "interactive media" is associated with limited neurological activity . . . real-world cognitive demands – especially early ones – physically improve and enlarge children's brains.'[4] So although most settings will not invest in a Wii or similar equipment, it is worth practitioners remembering that children who spend a lot of out-of-school time in such activities may exhibit some unexpected behaviours or traits.

Work/play dimensions

There is an implied importance to the word 'work,' in contrast to the word 'play,' which is probably why, all those years ago, Susan Isaacs coined the phrase about play being a child's work. But times and knowledge have moved on: we now know that play is *not* a child's work but a child's play: a sometimes serious but often fun activity for young children through which they experience life, love and happiness and, on the way, learn much.

Neither is play just a preparation for life at work: although children may mimic adult roles in their pretend play, they are playing in the here and now and not practising for an (unknown) future.

> Play is always an adaptation of the world to the self, while work is always an adaptation of the self to the world ... for both children and adults, play is a healthy counterpoise to work; and the two should not be equated.[5]

Play is a preoccupation rather than an occupation!

Yet, it seems that even for children's play characters – like Bob the Builder, the Fat Controller and SpongeBob Squarepants – work must dominate: previously, cartoon characters never let their work get in the way of playing and having fun.[6]

Play has been well identified in earlier parts of this book as self-chosen and intrinsically motivating. Work is sometimes self-chosen and sometimes motivating in itself but it is always intended to be productive, whereas children's play is a process and rarely has any product outcomes other than pleasure (see Diagram W1). Work is generally organized and systematic whereas play, by nature, is chaotic and flexible. The fact that children's learning is an outcome of play and playful experiences is indisputable but that is not their intention when playing. Children play to experience life, to learn about themselves and others, to test out emotions and allay fears ... and much more.

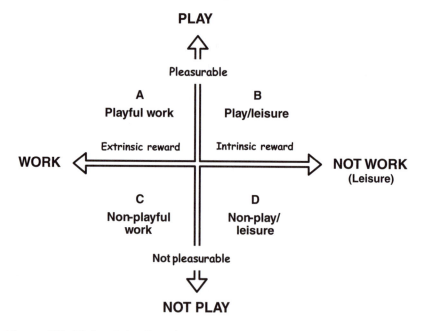

Diagram W1 Work and play dimensions

The intention in work is to make something – even if it is 'only' money! However, for many adults, work and play boundaries can be readily blurred (A in Diagram W1): the coping strategy of playful humour (often dark) and joking around among groups of police, fire-fighters and ambulance personnel who regularly deal with the harsher side of life shows how important that playful approach is. Those whose job it is to create something new, whether it be artefacts or ideas, must play mentally in order to achieve their intentions; for example, writers play with words in order to create new and unique texts be it prose or poetry.

Those who enjoy their work tend to be those who are most playful in carrying it out: those who cannot see play and playfulness often find work a chore and disappointing.[7]

> Play isn't a character defect: it's the builder of character, developing persistence, competence, mastery and social skills that take us beyond perceived limitations ... engaged play is the gateway not to time-wasting but to times that let you contact deeper realms ... Play satisfies core self-determination needs, such as autonomy and competence, as little else can ... You tap the true you, not the performance identity of the job or the presentation identity that we display to others. Play relieves you of the burden to be someone you're not ... Just you.[8]

If engaging in play and being playful is this important to adults with all their experiences, why is it that adults insist that children should 'work' rather than play? The answer is: to achieve outcomes determined by others who do not necessarily consider young children and their current childhood as important and insist on forcing them into adult work modes before it is appropriate. The role of practitioners is to understand children's deep engagement in the process of play and to defend it against those who do not understand its importance in children's lives now.

Children themselves well understand the difference for them conceptually between work and play. In one study, children were able to map activities on a play/work continuum.[9] Another study indicated that self-selection and choice were key for children in perceiving an activity as play; for example, a teacher-directed colouring task could be categorized as work whereas a self-initiated colouring activity could be regarded as play.[10]

References

1. Lanningham-Foster, L., Jensen, T., Foster, R., Redmond, A., Walker, B., Heinz, D. and Levine, J. (2006) Energy expenditure of sedentary screen time compared with active screen time for children, *Pediatrics*, 118(6): 1831–35.

2. Sigman, A. (2007) *Remotely Controlled: How Television Is Damaging Our Lives*. London: Vermilion.
3. Rideout, V., Vandewateer, S. and Wartella, A. (2003) *Zero-to-Six: Electronic Media in the Lives of Infants, Toddlers and Preschoolers*. Washington, DC: Henry J. Kaiser Family Foundation and the Children's Digital Media Centers.
4. Sigman, A. (2011) Does not compute, revisited: screen technology in early years education. In R. House (ed.) *Too Much, Too Soon? Early Learning and the Erosion of Childhood*. Stroud: Hawthorne Press (p. 267).
5. Elkind, D. (2001) *Thinking About Children's Play*. Redmond, WA: Child Care Information Exchange. Redmond, WA. Available online at www.web.mac.com/sharondeleon/FC/CDES_115_files/thinking_about_childrens_.pdf (accessed 30 January 2012).
6. Elkind, D. (2007) *The Power of Play*. Philadelphia, PA: Da Capo Press (p. x).
7. Terr, L. (2001) *Beyond Love and Work: Why Adults Need to Play*. New York: Touchstone/Simon & Schuster.
8. Robinson, J. (2010) *Don't Miss Your Life: Find More Joy and Fulfillment Now*. New York: Wiley.
9. Howard, J. (2002) Eliciting young children's perceptions of play, work and learning using the activity apperception story procedure, *Early Child Development and Care*, 172(5): 489–502.
10. Wiltz, N. and Klein, E. (2001) What do you do in child-care? Children's perceptions of high and low quality classrooms, *Early Childhood Research Quarterly*, 16(2): 209–36.

X Y Z

Xbox

Xbox is outside the age range for those players under age 7 (the main focus of this book). While it has been given credit for enabling communication between primary age children and above, communication for young children needs to be face to face so that they gain a greater understanding of body language and inter- and intra-communicational aspects.

Play could be said to offer 'xcitement,' 'xcellence' in 'xperiences,' 'xpectations' of fun and pleasure and 'xtensive xuberance' – but we will not dwell on those!

Young children

Young children need play. They also need the company of other young people of their own age group, above and below. Having younger children to play with shows slightly older children how much they have matured and gives them self-confidence. Playing with older children can teach younger ones a great many skills and encourages them to strive for greater understanding. Older children can be just the scaffold that young children need at certain stages in their learning.

Youth play

Youth play is outside the age range of this book but it is worth mentioning that much youth play is more competitive and more dangerous than young children's play, with risk being a major factor in the teenage years. Many teens seem to think that they are indestructible and will 'play' to the extreme for the high that it gives them and so as not to appear 'uncool' to their peers, especially boys. Healthy risk-taking is not only important in itself but can help prevent unhealthy risk-taking. Studies suggest that if young children are given more opportunities for challenging play, then they are more likely to understand the risks they are taking with over-the-top experiences as teenagers.

Zero-in on play

Zero-in on young children's play and you will be left in no doubt about its importance to them in their learning and other aspects of development. Play is also a natural way for practitioners to link with children in their own zones of play and to capitalize on children's playfulness to foster learning across the curriculum.

Photograph X1   Let's play!

Zigler

Zigler (Edward), the founder of Head Start, is an American psychologist who has studied children's play and development for many years and in many ways. His current concern is how much playful practice is being replaced in US preschools by:

> lessons focused on cognitive development, particularly literacy and reading, to match the content of standardized testing … We are not allowing normal, creative, interactive play … a child who begins kindergarten knowing letters and sounds may be cognitively prepared, but if he or she does not understand how to listen, share, take turns, and get along with teachers and classmates, this lack of socialization will hinder further learning … Four decades of research and practice, offer unequivocal evidence for the critical importance of play for children's development.[1]

His latest book examines play and children's reading and the vital role of play in supporting children's literacy learning.[2]

References

1. Zigler, E. and Bishop-Josef, S. (2006) *The Cognitive Child v. The Whole Child: Lessons from Forty Years of Head Start*. Available online at www.udel.edu/~ roberta/play/Zigler_Bishop.pdf (accessed 3 February 2012) (pp. 1, 13, 14).
2. Zigler, E., Singer, D. and Bishop-Josef, S. (2004) *Children's Play: The Roots of Reading*. Washington, DC: Zero To Three National Centre for Infants, Toddlers and Families.

Author Index

Subject Index

ENGAGING PLAY

Liz Brooker and Suzy Edwards (Editors)

978-0-335-23586-5   (Paperback)
2010

eBook also available

This insightful edited collection brings together the perspectives of leading and emerging scholars in early childhood education and play from within Europe, the UK, Australia, New Zealand and the USA.

The chapters cover a wide range of contexts, from child-led activity in informal settings to the more formal practice of school-based learning. A range of theoretical viewpoints of play are considered and related to the experiences of today's families, children and educators across different educational settings.

Engaging Play offers an insight into the pedagogical play discourse of twenty-first century early childhood education, and in doing so offers an informative reading experience for students, researchers and policy makers alike.

www.openup.co.uk

OPEN UNIVERSITY PRESS
McGraw - Hill Education

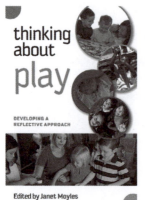

Edited by Janet Moyles

THINKING ABOUT PLAY

Janet Moyles (Editor)

978-0-335-24108-8   (Paperback)
2010

eBook also available

This edited collection brings together play and reflective practice and supports practitioners in reflecting more deeply on the play provision they make for young children. This involves analysing and evaluating what makes quality play and learning experiences by considering how current research might impact on practice.

Key features:

- Introduces the concept of 'playful pedagogies' and explains how it relates to practice
- Each chapter starts with an abstract so that readers can dip into issues of particular interest and concern
- Includes questions and follow-up ideas that can be used for CPD experiences and training

This important book supports early years students and practitioners in developing their own thinking, ideologies and pedagogies.

www.openup.co.uk

OPEN UNIVERSITY PRESS
McGraw · Hill Education